The Father's Heart For Prodigals

A 40-Day Prayer Journey

Lynn Holzinger

THE FATHER'S HEART FOR PRODIGALS
Copyright © 2018 by Lynn Holzinger.

Unless otherwise noted, Scripture quotations are taken from The Holy Bible, New International Version. Copyright © 1973, 1978, 1984, 2011 by Biblica, Inc. Used by permission.

Scripture quotations marked NLT are taken from The Holy Bible, New Living Translation. Copyright © 1996, 2004, 2015 by Tyndale House Foundation. Used by permission.

Scripture quotations marked NASB are taken from the New American Standard Bible. Copyright © 1960, 1962, 1963, 1968, 1971, 1973, 1977, 1995 by The Lockman Foundation. Used by permission.

All rights reserved. No part of this publication may be reproduced, stored in a retrieval system, or transmitted in any form by means electronic, mechanical, photocopying, recording or otherwise, except for the inclusion of brief quotations in a review, without prior permission in writing from the publisher.

ISBN: 978-0-692-95632-8

Published by
FATHER'S HEART PUBLISHING
EDWARDS, ILLINOIS

Front Book Cover: Joshua Betterton
Editing and proofreading: Lois Mannaioni

DEDICATION

*This book is dedicated to my son, who
I love with all my heart. I will always pray
for you and root for you. Thank you for giving
me your permission to publish this book.*

Contents

Introduction		7
1	In the Silence	13
2	God's Plans	16
3	Restored By God	19
4	The Prayer of the Righteous	21
5	Wanting What God Wants	24
6	Open Their Eyes Lord	27
7	The God of Second Chances	30
8	Love Keeps No Record of Wrongs	33
9	Perfect Love Drives Out Fear	37
10	Lord, You Say	41
11	A New Heart	45
12	God Must Be First	48
13	You Understand	52
14	Just Say the Word	55
15	He Broke Away Their Chains	59
16	Small Beginnings	63
17	A Ray of Hope	66
18	God's Arm is Not Too Short	69
19	The Beauty of Prayer and Praise	75

20	Light Their Path	70
21	No Shame	83
22	The Years the Locusts Have Eaten	86
23	The "Breaker Up"	90
24	We Wait for You	93
25	Jesus Is the Light	97
26	Tenderly	100
27	God's Armor	104
28	God Is and God Will	107
29	Yet I Will	111
30	Oh Lord, How Long?	115
31	Immeasurably More	119
32	The Shepherd	123
33	Your Plan for My Child	126
34	A Strong Tower	130
35	All Things are Possible	133
36	Two Lions	137
37	Determined by God	141
38	Being Sifted	145
39	Our War	148
40	Remaining Faithful	152
Acknowledgments		157

Introduction

I am blown away by the Father's Heart! It wasn't always so.

Although no one would have classified me as a prodigal because I went to church faithfully, served in the children's ministry, and even led a women's small group...I was dead inside. I had never experienced my heavenly Father's love and I knew it. I occasionally talked to God, but felt my prayers always hit the ceiling. My walk with Him was chaotic and heart-wrenching. For me, I truly encountered the Father when I was finally willing to deal with my total disappointment and disillusionment with God.

I screamed one day at two ladies who were praying with me, "What difference does it make if God loves me? I want people to love me"

I'm in tears as I write this. I am remembering this precious moment as I was sitting in the living room of the home of one of these dear women. Everything was about to change. Over the next few weeks I began to encounter the Father's heart and His absolute all-encompassing love for me. I was wrecked. His love was so much more than I could have ever imagined.

I still struggle with wanting the approval of others, but I am a work in progress. Psalm 63:3 says, *"Because Your lovingkindness is better than life, my lips will praise You."* This is now real to me.

So when my son told me he no longer believed in God, I was crushed. I went through all the normal responses that a mom would go through...*what did I do wrong? How could this happen? God, didn't I thank You over and over for my children following You in spite of the mistakes I made? I deserve this?*

I had no right to expect God to protect my children, especially my oldest one who suffered the most from my problems. All of these things rushed through my mind, but God has shown me He has not abandoned my son, and this happened for a reason. God is never surprised or at a loss. He is always in control. The Lord has taught me so much on this journey of faith.

Because my son lives so far away, I prayed and hoped spiritual detachment was a short phase. I didn't see or even talk to him very often, so at times my heart would be overwhelmed with grief and sorrow.

Three years ago, our pastor preached a sermon series on prayer, using Mark Batterson's book, *Draw the Circle*. Prayer came alive to me in ways it hadn't before. I started to understand why it is so important for us to pray and how much prayer can accomplish.

In our culture, we want to be in control; we want to fix what is broken. It's hard for us to not be able to change what we have no control over. It's difficult to give everything completely over to God. But when your loved one decides to walk away from what they believed, there is very little we can do to change them. It is their decision. Only God can transform a heart. We can continue to love and accept them for who they are, but as far as convincing them to come back to their heavenly Father, we can't do it...only God can.

So I began a journey of prayer and listening to the Lord. As I was reading through Mark Batterson's book, I read about a women who had started a 40-day prayer challenge with other moms who also had prodigal children. God impressed on me to begin a similar group. It wouldn't be exactly the same, but its main focus would be prayer. So I formed a group of 12 women who would commit to praying for each other's children for a period of 40 days. I would write a daily devotional and send it out by email. At the end of the 40 days, we decided to keep the group going, believing God for answers if we would continue praying and not give up.

Last summer, we did another 40-day Prayer Challenge and the devotions I wrote for the group have now become this book. We have seen many miraculous answers to prayer and two daughters and one son completely return to the Lord. For this we give Him praise!

We have added several more people to the group and continue to grow, for which we are thankful! And now, being able to share these devotionals, many more individuals will hear about the importance of prayer and the Father's love for our dear prodigals.

My desire for you as you join me on this journey is that you will be encouraged. You will see the Father's heart—that your faith will grow and you will commit to praying for as long as it takes. I believe you will see answers to your prayers and find hope. I pray you will hear from the Father and know how much He loves your prodigal and you will be renewed to walk with

Him every step of the way.

> *In everything, by prayer and petition,*
> *with thanksgiving, present your requests to*
> *God. And the peace of God, which transcends*
> *our understanding, will guard our hearts*
> *and minds in Christ Jesus.*
> – Philippians 4:6

As we begin, it is important that we are united in our purpose and commitment to praying for our prodigals. Each one has a different story, but each story is close to God's heart.

We are embroiled in a war. The enemy has plans and strategies. So it only makes sense that we also have plans and strategies. But how do we know what to do? We go to the Lord. We listen to the Holy Spirit. We read the Word. We share with each other. God has a word for each one of us.

He has a unique plan for you:

- Ask Him for specific verses
- Put on your armor for protection and engagement
- Use your weapons of praise and the Word

- Learn the value of fasting
- Be persistent
- Stay in close communion with the Lord
- Ask God for direction
- Ask Him for something new and fresh
- Don't give in to discouragement
- Wait with expectation
- Ask God for wisdom
- Pray persistently

My heavenly Father has been very good to me. He has given me many promises for my son. I haven't seen them all become reality yet, but if God has said it, it will happen. Every day, I tell the Lord I trust Him with this. In turn, He gives me peace. I sometimes fret over things, but not so much about my son. God has got this! Thankfully, He is in control.

– Lynn Holzinger

Prayer Challenge – Day 1

IN THE SILENCE

When he came to his senses...
– Luke 15:17

Have you ever thought about how or what made the prodigal son finally come to his senses? We know his circumstances changed. Once he was embracing a lavish lifestyle full of pleasure and wild living, but then his money ran out. There was a famine in the land and he began to find himself in need (Luke 15:14). So, he took a job feeding pigs.

Here he was all alone with the swine. His friends were gone and he had nothing to distract him. He was hungry—and that's when it happened. He had a realization; God opened his eyes and he saw things for what they really were.

Is it possible this occurred because of the silence? He finally had time to think. As long as he had distractions and comforts, he didn't realize he was missing anything. He thought he had it all! Life was good—and now everything had changed. In his solitude, he had time to think, time to reflect and see what his life had become.

We all want our children to have happy and fulfilling lives, but have you ever stopped to think that as long as our wayward child's life is good, they may not see their need for God? They will not have a reason to change anything? Don't we want, most of all, for them to come to their senses? To have a sudden awakening? This often happens when God removes those distractions; those things they turn to for satisfaction. They are then left alone and in silence. They are in a position to hear God speak and see what He wants them to see...that life apart from Him is meaningless.

We most likely will struggle to pray that our loved one has to go as low as the Prodigal Son did before having a turnaround. But we need to ask God to intervene—to remove the noise, strip away the excuses and lies they use to drown out His voice.

We must let God decide what this means for our prodigals. Pray that the Lord puts them in a position which enables them to hear His voice saying, *"This is the way, walk in it"* (Isaiah 30:21)—and that these words that are living and active will pierce their souls and hit the mark. May our prodigals be startled with this realization and wake up!

I often talk to my heavenly Father while listening to music…songs that lead me into the presence of God; lyrics that have a message of hope and give me words to pray for our prodigals. One such example is *Awake My Soul* by Chris Tomlin. I may use it for myself as the song intends, or I may take some of the words and use them to intercede for others. As we sing along, we can ask God to touch the hearts of our prodigals; to breathe on them so they come alive; to resurrect their bones and for them to say, "I'm nothing without You, You're the only One who satisfies my soul."

Prayer Challenge – Day 2

GOD'S PLANS

*"For I know the plans I have for you,"
declares the Lord, "plans to prosper you
and not to harm you, plans to give you hope
and a future. Then you will call upon me and
come and pray to me, and I will listen to you.
You will seek me and find me when you seek me
with all your heart. I will be found by you," declares
the Lord, "and will bring you back from captivity. I
will gather you from all the nations and places
where I have banished you," declares the
Lord, "and will bring you back to the place
from which I carried you into exile."*
– Jeremiah 29:11-14

The first time I heard these verses was right after the birth of my second son. I was in the throes of depression. It was not really my habit to read the Bible but this day I was. I didn't understand what was happening to me and I guess I was looking for an answer. I was raised in the church and had attended Bible College, but to my knowledge, I had never heard these verses before. But suddenly, they jumped out at me.

Over the next 20 years, I heard verse 11 often. I can't say I really believed it, but there was a tiny glimmer of hope that He had given this passage to me. I look back now and know *for sure* this was true. But He also gave me verses 12-14!

I kind of stopped half way through verse 14 where God tells us, *"and will bring you back from captivity."* I wasn't sure how the rest applied.

The Jews of that day had been disobedient to the Lord. They did not follow Him and they ended up in captivity...much like our wayward children. Those verses are as true today for our prodigals as they were for me when I first heard them and as they were for the Jews back when they were prophesied by Jeremiah.

I thank God that He knows the plans He has for our children and that His plans are good. I trust that our prodigals will be convicted and call out and pray to Him. I know He will hear their cries because He says He will. I pray they will seek God with all their heart because they will find Him. He promises, *"I will be found by you. I will bring you back from captivity."*

This is what He did for me and this is what He will

do for our prodigals.

You may be thinking, "I don't see how my child will seek God," but never underestimate our great Creator. He is doing things in the heavenlies that we can't see. Our God can do anything and nothing is impossible with Him.

Right now, He is working and drawing our prodigals back into the fold. Our prayers are being heard. The plans God has are good...they are to prosper them and not to harm them! So keep seeking Him and never stop praying!

Prayer Challenge – Day 3

RESTORED BY GOD

He prays to God and finds favor with him, he sees God's face and shouts for joy; he is restored by God to His righteous state.
– Job 33:26

Is this verse the way you see your prodigal? If not, try to picture it in your mind's eye. It is important for us to see the end result and pray into it—to speak it back to the Lord and thank Him for His promise of restoration.

I believe our loving heavenly Father wants to restore each and every one of our prodigals and now is the time to pray without ceasing! Listen to what Jennifer LeClaire, Senior Editor of *Charisma Magazine*, and author of many books, writes:

> *This morning on our prayer line we were praying for the lost and a word of knowledge came forth about prodigal sons coming home. I've received a number of emails this morning from women on the call who said that word*

was for them. If you have a prodigal in your life, let's stand in agreement this morning that they are coming home to Jesus. The prodigals are on God's heart and on mine.

This isn't the first time I have heard this sentiment. It is going to take us standing in agreement and declaring whatever promises God gives us; speaking them aloud. Ask God for specific promises. He will give them to you if you are listening.

Praise God!

Here is what I see for my son. I picture the day when he (you can insert your prodigal's name):

- shouts out Your name from the rootop and proclaims that he is Yours
- sees all the good You have done for him
- knows You are the One who brought him to his knees
- lifts his hands to You because You set him free
- truly sees You and the beauty of Your worth
- knows that Your perfect grace has brought him to this place

(Taken from the song *Rooftops* by Jesus Culture)

Prayer Challenge – Day 4

THE PRAYER OF THE RIGHTEOUS

The prayer of the righteous man is powerful and effective.

– James 5:16

Prayer is one of the ways we release the will of God on the earth... *"Thy kingdom come, Thy will be done"* (Matthew 6:10).

When we know the Word of God, we know the will of God. When we listen to our heavenly Father, we understand His plans and desires for us. Praying His will is powerful and effective.

It is important to pray with understanding. Daniel was able to do this successfully because he knew the Word of God concerning his people. Darius had just become king. The Israelites had been in exile for 68 years and their banishment was close to ending. From his reading of Jeremiah 25:1-11, Daniel was able to know this, and of the sins that had led to the exile in the first place, as well as the consequences and length of time.

> *During the first year of his reign, I, Daniel, learned from reading the word of the Lord, as revealed to Jeremiah the prophet, that Jerusalem must lie desolate for seventy years. So I turned to the Lord God and pleaded with him in prayer and fasting. I also wore rough burlap and sprinkled myself with ashes.*
> – Daniel 9:2-3 NLT

What happened when he talked with God?

> *The moment you began praying, a command was given. And now I am here to tell you what it was, for you are very precious to God. Listen carefully so that you can understand the meaning of your vision.*
> – Daniel 9:23 NLT

Let me encourage you to read the entire account in Daniel 9. He identified with his people and offered a sincere and detailed prayer of confession.

Have you ever thought about identifying with the sins of your prodigal? I don't think Daniel personally committed any of the offences he was confessing:

"We have not listened to your servants the prophets..." (verse 6); *"All Israel has transgressed your law..."* (verse 11); *"We have not sought the favor of the Lord our God by turning from our sins and giving attention to your truth"* (verse 13).

After that he implores God to work on their behalf. Listen to what he asks:

- Verse 16— *"...in view of all Your faithful mercies, please turn your anger away from Jerusalem."*
- Verse 17— *"For your own sake, smile again on Your desolate sanctuary."*
- Verse 18— *"...we don't ask because we deserve it, but because You are so merciful."*
- Verse 19— *"O Lord, listen and act; do not delay, because your city and your people bear Your name."*

We must be bold and confident in what we ask because God is still the same God for us as He was for Daniel. He is still merciful, and we are a people who carry His name.

Prayer Challenge – Day 5

WANTING WHAT GOD WANTS

Now God had caused the official to show favor and sympathy to Daniel.
– Daniel 1:9

One thing I have noticed as I've been reading through the Bible this year is God's sovereignty and involvement in the world. The Almighty was always causing things to happen and people to react in certain ways. In this situation God prodded the official to show favor and sympathy to Daniel.

If you remember, Daniel was chosen as one of the young men to serve in King Nebuchadnezzar's palace. He was to be trained for three years and the young men would be assigned a daily ration of food. But Daniel was determined not to defile himself by eating the king's fare. When he asked the chief of staff's permission for him and his three friends to only eat vegetables and drink water, the man was reluctant because he knew the consequence for himself if the men grew weaker. But with God's blessing and the respect of the guard assigned to them by the chief of staff, they came to an agreement.

For 10 days, the young men would follow Daniel's diet. Daniel asked that they make their final decision based on how the men looked after this period of time.

At the end of the 10 days, they did indeed appear healthier than the rest of the young men who were following the king's diet. God received the glory.

The main point I want to share from this story is the role God played. With the Lord's favor, anything can happen—anywhere and at any time. God can use both believers and non-believers for His purposes. He can cause any person He chooses to show kindness to our prodigals in such a way that it results in God's glory being evident, and He uses the situation to soften and open their hearts.

We all desire what God wants for our prodigals and that is to love the Lord with all their heart, soul, mind, and strength.

May God's favor and mercy rest on each one of them as we pray for their return to the fold. May He cause someone else to look on them with kindness and compassion in a way that will give Him glory and bring our loved ones back. Like Daniel, we are determined to follow God's ways and we are standing in the gap for those we love.

Prayer Challenge – Day 6

OPEN THEIR EYES LORD

...to open their eyes, so they may turn from darkness to light and from the power of Satan to God. Then they will receive forgiveness for their sins and be given a place among God's people, who are set apart by faith in me."
– Acts 26:18 NLT

This verse was Paul's response to King Agrippa. The Jewish community had been complaining to Festus, the Roman governor of Judea, that they wanted Paul killed. But Festus had found nothing deserving of death, so he brought him before Agrippa to see what he had to say.

King Agrippa gave Paul permission to speak freely, and the apostle recounted his past and his conversion. In this passage we read in more detail what Jesus said to Paul on the road to Damascus. The verse above was part of his commission. After he was finished speaking, Agrippa also found nothing worthy of the ultimate punishment, so Paul was set free.

This verse is what I would like to focus on: *"...to open their eyes so they may turn from darkness to light and from the power of Satan to God."* That is what we are praying for. We know the enemy comes to steal, kill, and destroy, and we know he will take any advantage he can. He will deceive us at every turn and will try to devour anyone who gives him the slightest opportunity.

We cannot let Satan outwit us, and we need to be aware of his cunning schemes. We must put on the full armor of God, for our struggle is not against flesh and blood, but against the spiritual forces of evil and the powers of this dark world. We need to stand in the gap for our prodigals knowing with all our hearts that God is able to turn them from darkness to light. We must not allow the enemy to veer us off track.

It may appear that Satan has won, but make no mistake...we are a mighty force when we pray...God responds and when He is on our side, who can be against us?

Romans 8:38-39 says that nothing can stand in His way; nothing can separate us or our prodigals from

God's love...neither death, nor life, nor angels, nor principalities, nor things present, nor things to come, nor powers, nor height, nor depth, nor any other created thing, will be able to separate us from the love of God, which is in Christ Jesus our Lord.

Our heavenly Father's love is all-consuming; He is reaching out to our prodigals as we pray. And don't be mistaken, God will win!

Prayer Challenge – Day 7

THE GOD OF SECOND CHANCES

When they had finished eating, Jesus said to Simon Peter, "Simon son of John, do you truly love me more than these?" "Yes, Lord," he said, "You know that I love you." Jesus said, "Feed My lambs."
– John 21:15

This is a familiar story. Peter had denied Jesus three times and now Jesus is restoring him. He asked Peter three times if he loved Him, and three times Peter replied, "Yes!"

God is a God of second chances—and third chances, etc. We can never fall so far from His love and grace that we can't be redeemed.

In the Old Testament, the Israelites repeatedly turned away from their Creator. But time and time again, He called for their return and when they did, He always forgave and restored them. This is a picture of the mercy of God—and even in these perilous times, the Lord hasn't changed.

> *My dear brothers and sisters, if someone among you wanders away from the truth and is brought back, you can be sure that whoever brings the sinner back from wandering will save that person from death and bring about the forgiveness of many sins.*
> *– James 5:19-20 NLT*

One of my favorite parables is the Lost Sheep found in Luke 15:4-7. Jesus will diligently search for the one that has strayed, and verse 4 tells us He will not rest until He finds the one who is lost.

But I thought, *What is the point of my prayers if Jesus is going to find our prodigals anyway?* So I went to God, and this is what I heard Him speak to my heart:

> *Your prayers are for your child, Lynn...not to convince Me to go looking. The enemy is out to destroy them, distract them, and steal every ounce of their faith. They will keep wandering further and further away, but for your prayers*

that go up to My throne. Stopping the plans and tactics of the enemy leaves room for My grace to enter. You can look at it from two viewpoints: 1) Jesus out searching until they are found and 2) Your prayers serving as roadblocks to slow them down.

The whole point of the parable is for you to know with certainty that Jesus will find them. And the point of your prayers is to speed up the process by stopping the enemy and slowing down your child.

So, keep praying God's Word—boldly, out loud, consistently, persistently, passionately, coming before the throne of grace with confidence to receive mercy and grace for your prodigals in their time of need.

God is always listening; He is fighting for us. He is working; and is ready to give all who turn to Him a second chance.

Prayer Challenge – Day 8

LOVE KEEPS NO RECORD OF WRONGS

Love is patient, love is kind. It does not envy, it does not boast, it is not proud. It is not rude, it is not self-seeking, it is not easily angered, it keeps no record of wrongs.
– 1 Corinthians 13:4-5

Our prodigals may have given us plenty of reasons to keep or not keep a record of misdeeds ...some more than others.

It is easy to live in the disappointment and forget that God is working all things together for good for those who love Him (that being us). It's hard to keep our eyes focused on Jesus when our prodigal is so blatant or indifferent. However, God has called us to pray, not to be their Holy Spirit. He has called us to remember the end result, not the current situation.

I have a strained relationship with my son, and he shares very little of his life with me. I could take it personally, but since he has two brothers who aren't much different in regards to sharing details of their daily lives (and they are still following Christ), I suspect it has more to do with being a guy then trying to hide a godless lifestyle. So I may not have a good understanding of how difficult it is to live with this, or to have dealt with it for a long time. But God knows and that's what matters.

I came across an article that includes a book review of *Come Back Barbara* written by Jack Miller (pastor, evangelist, author and founder of Harvest Mission) and his returned prodigal daughter, Barbara. He is very honest about the struggles he and his wife had dealing with their daughter and what he discovered along the way, and she shares what drew her back after 10 years of wandering. The following includes a few things they learned:

Jack: "I was trying to be the Holy Spirit in Barbara's life, and in doing so I only succeeded in making her more aware of me than of God."

Barbara: "The conflict between us allowed me to continue to blame my parents, not my own choices, for the pain in my life."

Jack: "When we are trying to press a situation and do the work in someone's life that only the Holy Spirit can do, we are revealing our own unbelief and lack of trust in God's plan and timing."

Barbara: "The more my parents were able to love me for who I was, instead of who they wanted me to be, the more I was drawn back into relationship with my family. And it was the reconnecting with my family that God used to slowly draw my heart back to Him."

Jack: "The practice of comprehensive forgiveness overcomes our own love of being right, our actual enjoyment and treasuring of our sense of being wronged...frustrated condemnation of others and the treasuring of old wrongs are not part of the artillery of God but the slithering, slimy, deadly creatures of the Prince of Darkness."

Michelle Mayer, the author of this book review, (and one who also has a prodigal) goes on to say:

> *Until we can trust God by letting go of the hurts and betrayals our own children have inflicted upon us, and entrust our hearts and theirs to His care, we will not feel free to love*

them in the way God calls us to love them. We will not feel strong enough or brave enough. Hurts quite naturally cause us to want to protect ourselves.

When we can love them in this way, we will not keep a record of wrongs. I confess that although I love my son, and it is not that difficult for me...I have not had to deal with a smidgen of what some of you have had to endure.

I know you love your prodigals or you would not be reading this book. But as I was writing this, I realized I have some work of my own to do. Since this is the case (and I haven't had it so tough), then you who are having an extremely difficult time because your prodigal has made bad decision after bad decision need special encouragement or stragegies. Perhaps he or she has continued to hurt you with verbal assaults, lying, irresponsibility or self-centeredness. May you be able to love your child as God does.

He is faithful to do what He says!

Prayer Challenge – Day 9

PERFECT LOVE DRIVES OUT FEAR

There is no fear in love. But perfect love drives out fear, because fear has to do with punishment. The one who fears is not made perfect in love.
— 1 John 4:18

Recently I had a dream—one of those kind that lingers on. The dream itself wasn't bad but it left a kind of uneasy feeling inside as I went through my day.

I wanted so badly to be strong and turn to God, but I failed initially. After work, I turned to my "crutch" …TV. When will I learn to turn to God immediately?

I cried out, "I am so sorry, Lord" for what seemed like the millionth time, "Will you please forgive me? And teach me to remember that You are the answer?"

Why am I sharing this with you? Well, it struck me that no matter how many times I fail, I do not fear going to God and asking for His forgiveness. I know utterly and completely that He loves me. There is no fear. I am not afraid of punishment because God knows my heart. Living in His love is what makes me unafraid.

However, this is not the place our prodigals are. The principle is the same for them but they don't believe it is true. On our worst days, we may struggle to believe it also. And for the record, I am not implying TV is wrong, but sometimes it can be when it replaces turning to God for what we need. Allow me to take the verse above in three directions:

First…God's love and our prodigals.

Our wayward children aren't living in His love, or at least the awareness of it. Does this change the fact that God loves them? No, it doesn't. Can God make them aware? Absolutely. It's one of the things I pray for…that they are mindful of His love and that they would realize how high and wide and deep and long it is.

I pray that they would experience His care and compassion in a real way and be drawn to it, and that His love would make them unafraid to cry out to Him.

This is a prayer God longs to hear. There will be no punishment, only forgiveness and joyfulness. But as long as they are living far from His will, they will not run to Him; their hearts must be touched by His love.

Second...Our love and our prodigals.

We want to create an atmosphere that says to our prodigal—"I love you and although I will not compromise my beliefs, I will allow you to live your life the way you choose. I see you and all your potential. My love for you will not waver and when you are ready, I will be here. I long for your return because I know first hand what living in God's love is all about. There is nothing better. But as long as you don't see it that way, I will pray and ask the Lord to deal with you in His way and in His time."

Our love may not be perfect, but God can and will intervene and cover our imperfections if we are living as He planned. He will not let us be put to shame.

Go to God with prayer and praise. Push back the darkness and refuse to be intimidated by the enemy, Lean into Jesus; trust His timing and know He is working. Ask God to lead you and show you how to love your prodigal in such a way that you are joining with Him in what He is doing. You are working together for the same end. Believe your prayers are moving heaven and earth.

Third...God's love and us.

There is no fear in love. When we give into our apprehension, worry, or regret and let those things take us down a path that does not include God's love, power, and authority, we have forgotten who He is. We have taken our eyes off of Jesus and put them on our circumstances or ourselves.

Of course, as I have learned personally, this can happen. You may even get sick of it taking place. But please don't fear God's love. He will always long for you and your return even if you only left for an afternoon.

Remember, there is no fear in love!

Prayer Challenge – Day 10

LORD, YOU SAY

But You have said, "I will surely make you prosper and will make your descendants like the sand of the sea, which cannot be counted."
– Genesis 32:12

This is a promise God had given to Jacob, and now Jacob was preparing to meet Esau. He had no idea how to approach his brother, and verse 7 says he went, "in great fear and trembling..." Jacob had reason to be afraid because years earlier he had deceived their father and received the blessing that rightly belonged to Esau.

On hearing what he had done, Esau threatened to kill Jacob, but their mother found out and told him to flee to Haran and stay with her brother Laban. He journeyed there and ended up marrying two of Laban's daughters, and became quite wealthy.

Jacob learned of Laban's sons complaint about his wealth and noticed that Laban's attitude toward him had changed. God instructed Jacob to return to his home and promised to be with him. He had quite a time getting away, and Laban wasn't happy because his daughters had now departed with Jacob.

Remembering his brother's threats, Jacob prepared to meet him. It was an elaborate plan. At one point he sent messengers ahead and when they returned they told him Esau was on his way to meet him.

Jacob was afraid Esau still wanted to kill him. So he went to the Lord and began to remind God of all the things He had said to him: "God, you told me to go back and that you would prosper me. I know I am not worthy of your kindness and faithfulness. But I am asking you to save me from the hand of my brother if he attacks me, my wives, and our children. You have promised to make my descendants like the sands of the sea."

Then Jacob continued with his plan. As it turned out, Esau was delighted to see his brother and Jacob didn't need to be afraid. God was faithful!

What promises has the Lord given us? Plenty! Here are just a few:

- Lord, You say, *"I will do whatever you ask in My name, so that the Son may bring glory to*

the Father. You may ask Me for anything in My name and I will do it" (John 14:13-14).
- Lord, You say, *"Whatever you ask for in prayer, believe that you have received it, and it will be yours"* (Mark 11:24).
- Lord, You say, *"Believe on the Lord Jesus Christ and you will be saved—you and your household"* (Acts 16:31).
- Lord, You say, *"Delight yourself in the Lord, and He will give you the desires of your heart"* (Psalm 37:4).
- Lord, You say, *"You are able to do immeasurably more than all we ask or imagine, according to the power that is at work within us"* (Ephesians 3:20).
- Lord, You say, *"Train up a child in the way he should go and when he is old, he will not depart from it"* (Proverbs 22:6).
- Lord, You say, *"He who began a good work in you will carry it on to completion until the day of Christ Jesus"* (Philippians 1:6).
- Lord, You say, *"For it is God who works in you to will and to act according to His good purpose"* (Philippians 2:13).

- Lord, You say, *"I will fight those who fight you and I will save your children"* (Isaiah 49:25 NLT).
- Lord, You say, *"All your sons will be taught by the Lord, and great will be your children's peace"* (Isaiah 54:13).
- Lord, You say, *"The descendants of the righteous will be delivered"* (Proverbs 11:21 NASB).

Heavenly Father, help each of us today to *"diligently study the Scriptures"* (John 5:39) so that we will continue to find more promises, and those that are written for our prodigals, speak them to our hearts. As we read Your Word, may a particular scripture jump out at us. Give us one word for our prodigal and then lead us to verses that pertain to them using that word.

Give us strength and faith to pray persistently and never give up.

Prayer Challenge – Day 11

A New Heart

I will give you a new heart and put a new spirit in you; I will remove from you your heart of stone and give you a heart of flesh. And I will put My Spirit in you and move you to follow My decrees and be careful to keep My laws.
– Ezekiel 36:26-27

In Day 4 we talked about how the Israelites had been held in captivity for 68 years, and that Daniel identified with and confessed the sins of his people.

The prophet Ezekiel was also a captive in Babylon and, in 593BC, was called by God to proclaim an almost identical message that Jeremiah had been given—that Israel's sinfulness would lead to the destruction of Jerusalem. Neither the exiles in Babylon or those who were left in Jerusalem believed his message. So, in 586BC, when Jerusalem was destroyed, the people were shocked, and soon in despair. They felt abandoned by God and said, *"Our sins are heavy upon us, we are wasting away! How can we survive?"* (Ezekiel 33:10 NLT). That's when God gave Ezekiel a new message to give to the people. It was one of hope and restoration. God would give them back their land and make them more prosperous than they were before. He would give them a new heart to obey and put a new spirit in them to follow God's decrees.

This is also a perfect picture of what God will do for our prodigals. Like Israel, they have abandoned God. But the Lord's love for them hasn't changed. His mercy is alive and well. He has a plan for them, and He knows how to get their attention and what they need.

In the Old Testament we read of two separate prophets who ran from God for two different reasons, and God responded differently to each one. Jonah fled because he didn't want to obey what the Lord asked of him, so the Almighty sent a storm and a big fish.

Elijah ran because he was afraid. He took his eyes off God and put them on his circumstance. He was ready to give up! The Lord sent an angel to minister to him and food to strengthen his body. Nothing ever takes the Lord by surprise and nothing can stop His plans.

God knows our prodigals better than they know themselves, and He has the ability to reach them at the right moment. We don't have to worry; we have to pray. Even though our prodigals are running, they can't outrun God!

Remember, our prayers are like roadblocks that slow our prodigals down and frustrate the plans the enemy has for them. Our prayers are also a way for us to declare to God His promises, as we talked about in Day 10. The prayers of the righteous are powerful and effective (James 5:16).

Prayer Challenge – Day 12

GOD MUST BE FIRST

*But seek ye first the kingdom of
God, and His righteousness, and all these
things shall be added unto you.*
– Matthew 6:33 KJV

Sometimes we get so caught up in praying for our prodigals that we neglect to call on God first. We forget that seeking the Lord is more important than anything else. He is the One who knows what is really going on in our prodigal's life and in the spiritual realm. He will share some of this with us as we spend time in His presence so we can have hope and faith; so we can pray more effectively and claim the promises He speaks to our heart, but we do not see the whole picture.

Seeking Him first and giving Him glory sets us up to know how to pray. Even more significant, it allows us to know Him intimately. As a result, we will love and trust Him completely...with our lives and with the lives of our loved ones.

> *He must become greater; I must become less.*
> *– John 3:30*

> *Jesus replied, "Love the Lord your*
> *God with all your heart and with all your*
> *soul and with all your mind."*
> *– Matthew 22:37*

> *"I am the vine; you are the branches. If a*
> *man remains in me and I in him, he will bear much*
> *fruit; apart from me you can do nothing."*
> *– John 15:5*

> *Come, see the glorious works of the Lord:*
> *See how he brings destruction upon the world.*
> *He causes wars to end throughout the earth. He*
> *breaks the bow and snaps the spear in two; he burns*
> *the shields with fire. "Be still, and know that I am*
> *God! I will be honored by every nation. I will*
> *be honored throughout the world."*
> *– Psalm 46:8-10 NLT*

God wants us to seek Him *first* in everything. He desires for us to humble ourselves under His mighty hand because He is God and He has the answers—and it's the only way we are going to truly know His heart.

The more we know Him, the more we love and trust Him. Our confidence flows from above, not from ourselves. The following are some of the words God shared with me:

> *I know it is not easy to humble yourself; I made you. I know you intimately and I know that once sin entered the world that it would be difficult.*
>
> *I understand your weakness and I do not hold it against you. I look at your heart and your desire to please Me. You have died with Christ and He has set you free from the spiritual powers of this world. Little by little I am transforming you and you must keep seeking Me and not worry about the details—I will take care of those.*
>
> *The enemy hates your prayers and he despises even more that you are seeking Me because he knows he is defeated, and when you also know it, you will be able to resist him and hold Me in the place of honor that I deserve.*

The Father's Heart for Prodigals

When you spend time in My presence, you get to know My heart and My love for you, and for prodigals. You hear My words through Scripture, or in the still, quiet voice I speak to your heart, or through the beauty of creation.

I speak in a thousand different manners and I want you to know and experience Me in many ways. I want to speak to you about the love and compassion I have for prodigals. I care for them infinitely more than you do. I love them with an everlasting love that cannot be shaken or defeated. My compassions are new every morning...great is My faithfulness.

Prayer Challenge – Day 13

YOU UNDERSTAND

> *As He approached Jerusalem and saw the city, he wept over it and said, "if you, even you, had only known on this day what would bring you peace—but now it is hidden from your eyes."*
> – Luke 19:41-42

Sometimes we weep because, at the moment, we see that our children don't know what would bring them peace—just like Jesus did over Jerusalem in the passage above. This was His last visit before He would be crucified and He was overcome with emotion.

The Greek word here for weeping is 'klaio' which means *audible* weeping as opposed to the Greek word 'dakruo' used in the story of Lazarus' death which means to shed *silent* tears. Jesus was visibly and audibly crying.

The crowds were rejoicing and praising God. They were waving palm branches and spreading their cloaks on the road as the Son of God rode along on a donkey. We refer to this as Palm Sunday or His triumphal entry.

I've heard this story told dozens of times, but never really paid attention to Jesus' response as He approached Jerusalem. He was coming from the east side, on the road that went down the Mount of Olives.

When you reach the Kidron Valley, you overlook the city of Jerusalem. It is beautiful! If you have ever visited Israel, you know how magnificent this view is.

Jesus burst into tears because He knew what they *didn't* know. He understood what they were missing because of their unbelief and He could see what destruction lay ahead for them.

On another day, Jesus looked over Jerusalem and uttered these words: "I have longed to gather your children together, as a hen gathers her chicks under her wings, but you were not willing."

Jesus understands exactly how we are feeling because He has felt the same way. He is our high priest who is able to sympathize with our weaknesses—and our prodigal's weaknesses—because He has been there. Even now, He understands and longs for our wayward children to live in the light of His love and mercy...to know this love that surpasses knowledge—that they may be filled to the measure of all the fullness of God.

Jesus is God. Therefore He sees the future; we do not. Our tears are not for what we do not know, rather for what they are now missing. But Jesus saw the future for Jerusalem and He sees the future for our prodigals.

I can't tell you if He is weeping at this moment, but I do know that He identifies with us and that He hears our cries for mercy.

> *While Jesus was here on earth, he offered prayers and pleadings, with a loud cry and tears, to the one who could rescue him from death. And God heard his prayers because of his deep reverence for God. Even though Jesus was God's Son, he learned obedience from the things he suffered. In this way, God qualified him as a perfect High Priest, and he became the source of eternal salvation for all those who obey him.*
> – Hebrews 5:7-9 NLT

Prayer Challenge – Day 14

JUST SAY THE WORD

"…just say the word, and my servant will be healed."
– Matthew 8:8

Jesus had just returned to Capernaum when a centurion rushed over to the Lord and asked Him to heal his servant who was paralyzed and suffering terribly. Jesus said He would go and heal him. But the centurion told the Lord that he didn't deserve to have Him come under his roof—and if Jesus would just say the word, his servant would be healed.

The man explained that he understood authority because he himself was subject to a higher command and had soldiers under him. This centurion knew Jesus had power over sickness, disease, and injuries as well as death, nature, and demons. He no doubt had either witnessed or heard of Jesus healing others. Still, the Son of God was amazed to find a man with such great faith. He told the centurion to go home because it would be done just as he believed it would. And that very hour his servant was healed.

Just say the word, Lord! we pray. Just say the word and our prodigal's life will be changed forever.

What are you asking of Jesus? It's about boldly requesting what we want Him to do and then having the faith to believe that He is able. Yes, He is *"able to do immeasurably more than all we ask or imagine..."* (Ephesians 3:20).

In His encounter with the centurion, notice that Jesus didn't do what He said He would do (go and heal him) but He did what the centurion *believed* He could do.

Jesus alone is the One with all authority ...over salvation, healing, freedom, the church, rulers, powers, authorities, angels, and all people. God has given this supremacy to Him.

As He was praying in the Garden of Gethsemene before He was arrested and crucified, Scripture tells us:

> *"For you granted him [Jesus] authority*
> *over all people that he might give eternal*
> *life to all those you have given him."*
> – John 17:2

After His resurrection and just prior to His ascension:

> *"All authority in heaven and on*
> *earth has been given to me"*
> – Matthew 28:18

Now, seated at the right hand of God and in the future age:

> *[God's power] raised Christ from the*
> *dead and seated him in the place of honor*
> *at God's right hand in the heavenly realms. Now he*
> *is far above any ruler or authority or power or leader*
> *or anything else—not only in this world but also in*
> *the world to come. God has put all things under the*
> *authority of Christ and has made him head over all*
> *things for the benefit of the church. And the church*
> *is his body; it is made full and complete by Christ,*
> *who fills all things everywhere with himself.*
> – Ephesians 1:20-23 NLT

*[Christo has ascended] to heaven and is
at God's right hand—with angels, authorities
and powers in submission to him.*
– 1 Peter 3:22

Jesus loves our prayers and is amazed when we possess great faith!

Prayer Challenge – Day 15

HE BROKE AWAY THEIR CHAINS

He brought them out of darkness and the deepest gloom and broke away their chains.
– Psalm 107:14

Two times in the book of Acts, we have a record of chains literally falling off individuals. In Acts 12:6-11, Peter escapes from prison when suddenly an angel appears, strikes him on his side, wakes him up, and tells him to rise up. The chains fell from his wrists.

Then the angel instructed Peter to get dressed and wrap his cloak around himself and follow him. The disciple did as he was told, following him out of the prison, passing the first and second guards and coming to the iron gate leading to the city. Peter thought it was a vision—but it wasn't! The gate opened itself and they walked the length of one street before the angel departed, just as suddenly as he had appeared. Then Peter came to himself and realized it had actually happened, in real time.

The second account is described in Acts 16:25-34, when Paul and Silas were thrown in prison. They were singing praises to God at midnight while the other prisoners were listening, but the guard was asleep.

Unexpectedly, there was a violent earthquake and all the prison doors burst open. The guard woke up, saw what had happened and planned on killing himself because he thought the prisoners had all escaped. But Paul shouted "Stop! Don't harm yourself. We are all still here."

This led to the guard's salvation—not only his, but his whole family.

Our prodigals are bound by chains that can't be seen. They are held in a prison of their own making. This is why Jesus came to set them free.

> *"The Spirit of the Sovereign Lord is on me, because the Lord has anointed me to preach the good news to the poor. He has sent me to bind up the brokenhearted, to proclaim freedom for the captives and release from darkness for the prisoners..."*
> – Isaiah 61:1

Several years ago, I had been praying intently for a young man who was facing his own struggles. God gave me what I consider a vision. I saw the man sitting in a chair, completely tied up with chains. He wasn't resisting his confinement because he wasn't aware of the shackles. I kept praying.

After a while the vision changed. The young man realized that he was in chains and started struggling, but it was doing no good because he didn't have the keys and no one was around to help him. I kept praying.

The picture changed again and now he was no longer fighting back. He had surrendered. I kept praying.

Finally in the last scene of the vision, the chains had fallen from his body. He was a free man!

During this whole time I had no idea what was going on in his life. We had almost no contact since he moved away from our city. Today he is married to a godly woman and is following the Lord.

I share this with you because it is a picture of progression. Our prayers go to the throne of God and things change, even when we can't see what is taking place in the physical realm. But God is working.

It reminds me once again of the song *Rooftops* by

Jesus Culture that I shared in Day 3. It's envisioning the time when they are free, just like the young man I had been praying for. Let me paraphrase the lyrics, which anticipate the day when they:

> *Shout out Your Name; from the rooftops*
> *they proclaim, that they are Yours.*
> *See all the good You have done for them and*
> *You are the One who bought them to their knees.*
> *Lift their hands to You because You set them free.*
> *Truly see You and the beauty of Your*
> *holy worth.*
> *Know that Your perfect grace has brought*
> *them to this place.*

Prayer Challenge – Day 16

SMALL BEGINNINGS

Do not despise these small beginnings, for the Lord rejoices to see the work begin...
– Zechariah 4:10 NLT

The children of Israel had returned to Jerusalem after 70 years of exile in Babylon. Zerubbabel, the governor, along with the people, had laid the foundation for the temple, but then he and the workers became discouraged with the enormous task ahead and abandoned the project for nearly 20 years.

God raised up two prophets, Haggai and Zechariah, to encourage the people. Haggai challenged them to begin building again and they did, but spiritually, they were still corrupt. Then God called Zechariah to speak to the Israelites with kind, comforting words, encouraging them to return to the Lord with genuine repentance. The key verse above includes some of the words Zechariah received from the Lord. He told Zerubbabel not to despise the small beginnings.

God had acted in the past for their ultimate good, even in their exile, and the Lord would accomplish His purposes now.

Everything God does is for our benefit. He wanted patience and faith from His people then, and He desires the same from us today. We too, are not to make light of small beginnings, but to trust God. He knows what He's doing in our lives and in our prodigals' lives. Even when it looks overwhelming and we can't see any progress, we must stand on faith and reject the lie.

The truth is that God is working on our behalf. And keep in mind some other words spoken to Zerubbabel through the prophet Zechariah,

> *"Not by might nor by power, but by My Spirit" says the Lord Almighty.*
> – Zechariah 4:6

It's not about us doing all the "right things" —rather, it concerns the power of God's Spirit working in our prodigals' lives.

Instead of focusing on what we can't see or on all the things that need to happen and change:

- Focus on God
- Focus on the work of the Holy Spirit
- Focus on the finished work of Christ

We aren't building a temple; we are praying for the return of our prodigals. So let's be faithful to pray according to God's will—to seek His face persistently, for as long as it takes, knowing that God is faithful and He is working.

Small beginnings are good!

Prayer Challenge – Day 17

A RAY OF HOPE

The Lord will command His lovingkindness in the daytime; and His song will be with me in the night, a prayer to the God of my life.
– Psalm 42:8 NASB

The psalmist was depressed. He is remembering how wonderful it used to be. In verse 5, he begins to strengthen himself in the Lord:

Why am I discouraged? Why is my heart so sad? I will put my hope in God! I will praise Him again—my Savior and my God!
– Psalm 42:5

He's saying that even though he was disheartened, he would take his eyes off his circumstances and praise God. This doesn't just happen. For the rest of the Psalm and through Psalm 43 (which is a continuation of Psalm 42), we see him being indecisive, vacillating back and forth.

I don't know about you, but this is how it is in my

own life. The psalmist is going to God and pouring out his soul; going through the process of breaking out of the darkness and going toward the light.

He asks hard questions about God's perceived abandonment. This happens quite a few times in the Psalms. It's like journaling for me...a place where I can be honest and real, and then look to God for my hope and joy.

The Lord is faithful, but I don't always perceive it in the moment. He is constantly by my side, yet sometimes I can't sense His presence. It's a good thing truth doesn't revolve around our feelings. We can always go back to the Word of God for truth because it will give us a bright ray of hope.

We see the psalmist praying to Almighty God —struggling because of what is happening to him in the physical realm, but in the spiritual realm he can gain victory through praise and prayer. He doesn't have to be despondent; he doesn't have to live in fear, for he knows the One True God.

There will be times when we feel abandoned or without hope. We will wonder if God is listening to our prayers for our loved ones to return to Him. That's when we need to strengthen ourselves in the Lord... being reminded of who God is and what He has done.

T alk to yourself as the psalmist did, saying, "Why am I so discouraged? Why is my heart so sad? I will put my hope in God! I will praise Him for He is my Lord and my Savior."

Then start praying again, knowing that you are touching the heart of God, pushing back the darkness, and strengthening your relationship with your heavenly Father!

Prayer challenge – Day 18

GOD'S ARM IS NOT TOO SHORT

Surely the arm of the Lord is not too short to save, not his ear too dull to hear.
— Isaiah 59:1

Like so many people today, maybe even our prodigals, the Israelites wondered why God didn't save them from their troubles. Was He not able? Did He not have the power to end their suffering? Was His arm too short to save them? Did He not hear their cries?

How can a loving, all-powerful God let suffering continue? Maybe even you wonder why the Lord doesn't rescue your prodigal and bring them back immediately. At least in part, Isaiah speaks to this issue. The very next verse tells us:

But your iniquities have separated you from God; your sins have hidden his

face from you, so that he will not hear.
— Isaiah 59:2

These are God's chosen people whom He loved dearly. Yet He allowed them to choose their own path and make their own decisions. This is how He still operates.

- The problem isn't with God's power; the problem is with our sins

- The problem isn't that God doesn't care; the problem is our sins have hidden His face from us

How does our iniquity separate us from God? It certainly doesn't take us away from His presence because He is everywhere. And it doesn't distance us from God's love because Romans 5:8 tells us that God demonstrates His own love for us in that while we were still sinners, Christ died for us. So what does this mean?

- Sin separates us from **_fellowship_** with God, because when we are sinning, we are not thinking like God or communicating with Him.

- Sin separates us from the ***blessing*** of God because when we are transgressing, we are not thinking about the Lord or relying on Him.

- Sin separates us from the ***benefits of God's love*** because like the prodigal son, the Father still loved him, but while he was away, he could not enjoy the benefits of that love.

- Sin separates us from, in some ways, the ***protection*** of God because He will allow trials to come our way to draw us back. It will always be for our good and because He loves us and wants us to return. But never forget that the Lord will also allow us to suffer the results of our poor choices.

If we don't understand the consequences of sin, it is easier to blame God than the wrong things we do that results in separation. This is where our prodigals are now. The prophet Isaiah goes on to list the many wrongs the Israelites are guilty of, but then we come to verse 16.

> *He saw that there was no one, he was appalled that there was no one to intervene; so his own arm worked salvation for him, and his own righteousness sustained him.*
> *– Isaiah 59:16*

The Lord could not find one individual to intercede on their behalf so He did it Himself. He put on His own armor (verse 17) and went into battle—to destroy the enemy, protect His people, and glorify His name. Amazing!

God is looking for intercessors today, but when He doesn't find any, He will take action Himself because His plan will go forward...His purpose will be achieved. Notice that God put on His armor which parallels the armor Paul talks about in Ephesians 5:10-17. The armor of God prepares us for battle. He prefers to use us, but if He cannot find a candidate, it doesn't thwart His plans! And the end result will be wonderful! Please pay attention to verse 19:

> *From the west, men will fear the
> name of the Lord, and from the rising
> of the sun, they will reveal his glory. For
> he will come like a pent-up flood that
> the breath of the Lord drives along.*
> — Isaiah 59:19

There will be victory with or without us, but the Lord wants to use you and me so we can share in the victory. However we must remember, He is the One with the power! He does not need us in the sense that He is helpless without us. His arm is not too short! And when the enemy rushes in like a flood, he won't stand a chance.

I love the way the Kings James Version states the second half of verse 19: *"When the enemy shall come in like a flood, the Spirit of the Lord shall lift up a standard against him."*

Our adversary is no match for Almighty God!

I don't know about you, but it excites me that God uses our prayers in this way! That He is pleased because He sees there are people interceding for those who have fallen away. It makes me want to put on the armor that God has given us to use and battle for the souls of our prodigals.

    Amen!

Prayer Challenge – Day 19

THE BEAUTY OF PRAYER AND PRAISE

About midnight Paul and Silas were praying and singing hymns to God, and the other prisoners were listening to them.
– Acts 16:25

In Day 15, we talked about chains falling off prisoners and the story of Paul and Silas was mentioned. But today I want you to see what was taking place prior to that event.

It all started when Paul and Silas were going to the place of prayer (verse16). They were met by a slave girl who had an evil spirit of divination and made her owners a great deal of money. She kept following Paul and Silas for many days shouting that these men were servants of the Most High God and telling the way to be saved (this is not the first time that the Bible talks about demons telling the truth concerning who Jesus was (see Matthew 8:28-34 and Mark 3:11-12).

Finally, Paul became so annoyed that he commanded the spirit to come out of the young woman in the Name of Jesus. Immediately the spirit departed.

You can imagine how upset her owners were, realizing their means of making money was now gone. The angry owners seized Paul and Silas and brought them before the authorities, accusing them of inciting an uproar in the city. The crowd joined in and the town's officials had them beaten and thrown in prison.

Even after all they had gone through, Paul and Silas were praying and praising God in the night. And they weren't doing it quietly so as not to disturb or offend anyone because the other prisoners were listening to them. Then came the earthquake!

Do you think their praying and singing praises to the Lord had any connection to what God did? I'm convinced of it. I believe the Lord finds our prayers and praises to Him absolutely beautiful.

When Peter's chains fell off in Acts 12, verse 5 tells us the church was *"earnestly praying to God for him."*

So many times in the Bible and throughout history we find that praying plays a major role in the work of

God. As for praise, we see it over and over in Scripture, including singing to the Lord. Remember, the Psalms were written to be sung.

In 2 Chronicles 20:18-24, we find King Jehoshaphat appointing singers to walk ahead of the army, lifting their voices to God. They sang, *"Give thanks to the Lord; his faithful love endures forever!"*

Verse 22 tells us that at the very moment they began to voice their praise, God acted and they gained the victory.

Praying and praising are always our choice. When we feel defeated or downcast, God is right there beside us. When we need Him to intervene, He is listening and He will respond.

God alone is worthy of our worship, and when you feel least like praising Him, it is the very thing that will lift you into His presence.

> *Praise the Lord, for the Lord is good;*
> *sing praise to his name, for that is pleasant.*
> – Psalm 135:3

Offering praise gives God the glory due His name, and it also brings us joy. What else does it do? It silences the enemy.

> *From the lips of children and*
> *infants you have ordained praise*
> *because of your enemies, to silence*
> *the foe and the avenger.*
> – Psalm 8:2

This is the beauty of prayer and praise!

Prayer Challenge – Day 20

LIGHT THEIR PATH

***Your Word is a lamp to guide
my feet and a light for my path.***
– Psalm 119:105 NLT

The Word of God is living and active. It is sharper than any double-edged sword and exposes our innermost thoughts and desires. It is the Sword of the Spirit in our armor.

This "sword" is seen coming out of the mouth of Jesus at the second coming where His emphasis will be on judgement rather than mercy and grace (Revelation 1:16).

He uses this double-edged weapon to deliver a message to the church of Pergamum. The Lord addresses their spirit of compromise and urges them to repent or He will come to them suddenly and fight against them with the sword of His mouth (Revelation 2:12-16).

When the Lord returns to earth, He will strike down the nations. He will rule with an iron rod and release the full wrath of God Almighty, like juice flowing from a winepress (Revelation 19:15).

The Word of God will eventually bring judgement on earth, but right now, we are living in a period of grace, and grace is what is needed for our prodigals. It also is meant for us as we wait for the Lord to light their path.

God's Word is able to give us the wisdom to receive salvation; it teaches us what is true and makes us realize what is wrong with our lives. It corrects us when we stray and teaches us to do what is right.

Nothing compares to the awesome power of God's Word:

- It prepares and equips us to do every good work (2 Timothy 3: 15-16)
- It works in those who believe (1 Thessalonians 2:13)
- It helps us grow into maturity (1 Peter 2:2)

- It lives in our hearts and gives us power over the evil one (1 John 2:14)
- It gives us examples of how not to live (1 Corinthians 10:11)
- It will never disappear (Matthew 24:35)
- It protects our mind (Ephesians 6:17)
- It revives the soul, gives us wisdom, brings joy to our heart and gives us insight for living (Psalm 19:7-8)
- It gives us hope and encouragement as we wait patiently for God's promises to be fulfilled (Romans 15:4)
- It sets us free (John 8:32)
- It makes us holy (John 17:17)
- It points us to Jesus (John 20:31) who is the Word (John 1:1-5)

Our prodigals are on a path of darkness, but Christ is the light of the world (John 1:9; 6:12).

Lord, bring our prodigals Your Word that will expose the lies they believe, and replace those lies with the truth that will set them free. You have unlimited ways of bringing the Word they so desperately need to hear, so we ask You to shine Light on their path.

We will give You all praise and glory!

Prayer Challenge – Day 21

NO SHAME

As the Scripture says, "Anyone who trusts in him will never be put to shame."
– Romans 10:11

This is where the Israelites kept getting it wrong! God gave them laws to live by but they never got it right because they were trying to do things in their own strength rather than trusting in Him. When God sent Jesus to earth, they rejected His Son. He was the stone in Jerusalem that made them stumble. But anyone who puts their trust in Him will never be disgraced (Romans 9:30-33).

Just as the Israelites refused to accept God's way, so have our prodigals. They have decided to walk their own path. And just as God longed for the Israelites to return to Him, He has this same longing for our prodigals.

When we read what Paul wrote about the Israelites in Romans 11:11-15, we see that God had a purpose all along, and that was to offer salvation to the

Gentiles. The plan extended even further and included invoking jealousy in the Jews so they would claim salvation for themselves. This may happen in our day too! When the full number of Gentiles have accepted Christ, Jesus will come and turn Israel away from ungodliness (Romans 11:26).

Yes, Jesus can do that! And if He can cause an about-face of a whole nation from ungodliness, then I know He can cause a turnaround in our prodigals. And who's to say that His plan for them doesn't include their past? God doesn't waste any of our experiences to bring others back to the fold, or to salvation.

Lord, I see them standing faultless before the throne. You have removed their shame because they trust in You. They are standing before You holy in Your sight, blameless and free from accusation (Colossians 1:22). They are dressed in robes of righteousness. You remember their sins no more (Jeremiah 31:34).

God, even now, let them hear that You have not forgotten them. You have "swept away their offenses like a cloud, their sins like the morning mist." You say, "Return to Me, for I have redeemed you" (Isaiah 44:22).

The Father's Heart for Prodigals

Heavenly Father:

- You have summoned them by name, they are Yours (Isaiah 43:1)
- You will go before them and level the mountains, You will break down gates of bronze and cut through bars of iron so that they will know that You are the Lord.
- There is no other God apart from You

Strengthen them even though they do not acknowledge You so that from the rising of the sun to the going down of the same they will know that there is no one besides You...that You are the Lord and there is no other (from Isaiah 45:1-6).

There is no better place for our prodigals than in the palm of Your hand.

Prayer Challenge – Day 22

THE YEARS THE LOCUST HAVE EATEN

*I will repay you for the
years the locust have eaten...*
– Joel 2:25

God didn't want to inflict punishment. He loved His people, but He had to discipline them for their rebellion. His holiness demanded it and He had to capture their attention, so He sent the locusts to wipe out their crops. Then He instructed Joel to call them to repentance.

The prophet pleads for them to return to the Lord with the assurance that He is merciful and compassionate, slow to become angry and filled with unfailing love. He is eager to relent and not punish (Joel 2:13).

It is our heavenly Father's nature to forgive and

restore those who repent rather than judge and destroy.

God promises He will replace everything they lost because of the locusts. Then they would know, without a shadow of doubt, that He is the Lord their God, and that there is no other (Joel 2:27)

This is a vow for our prodigals as well. Right now the "locusts" are eating their years; the enemy is stealing them away. But God is calling our sons and daughters to repentance even as you read this. He is patient, slow to anger, and abounding in love. Our heavenly Father is sovereign and knows how to turn their heads toward Him. We don't know how long it will take, but we are committed to praying without ceasing.

Of course, we would love to see the answer today!

Even as our hearts break, we turn to You, God, because You are our hope and we know You are seeking them out. Your heart breaks too! Jesus, You came to proclaim freedom for the captives and release the prisoners from darkness (Isaiah 61:1).

You came to shine on those living without

light (Luke 1:79). We thank You in advance that You will give back the years the locusts have eaten when they return to You. You will restore the relationship they have lost, and they will bear much fruit. You are able to do immeasurably more than all we ask or imagine (Ephesians 3:20). God, may they hear Your voice today and return to Your loving arms.

The Lord deeply loves our prodigals. He will call them to repentance for a season, but at some point if they refuse to listen, He may have to bring a calamity to their lives to capture their attention. It is not what He desires to do, but maybe it's the only thing that will make them dissatisfied enough with their life and become willing to look elsewhere.

Then the Lord will send someone or "many someones" to speak God's words to them and they will be ready to listen. He may be placing a burden on believers right now to share His love, His compassion, and His Word with them.

It has been said that when a Christian is under an open heaven there is such an anointing on their life that when unbelievers or prodigals enter their presence there is less resistance and it is much easier to bring them to the cross.

May we be willing vessels to be used of God for these special assignments.

Prayer Challenge – Day 23

THE "BREAKER UP"

***One who breaks open the
way will go up before them...***
– Micah 2:13

God is the "Breaker Up." He opens up the way; He is the One who overcomes all obstacles.

Micah was another prophet God used to call the people to repentance, and his message was similar to other prophets. He was sent to Judah during the reigns of Jotham, Ahaz, and Hezekiah because the people were corrupt. Primarily, he warned of a future exile if they didn't listen, but also proclaimed restoration. Micah 2:13 is an example of this.

Our all-powerful, omnipotent God is ultimately in control. Here we see that He will gather His people together like sheep in a pen. He will go up before them; then they would break through the gate as He leads them out of exile.

There are other passages in Scripture that speak of Jesus as the Breaker Up, a term Jews were familiar with to describe the Messiah.

> *I, the Lord, have called you in righteousness;
> I will take hold of your hand. I will keep you and
> will make you to be a covenant for the people and a
> light for the Gentiles, to open eyes that are blind
> to free captives from prison and to release from
> the dungeon those who sit in darkness.*
> *— Isaiah 42:6-7*

> *The Lord will march out like a
> mighty man, like a warrior, he will stir up
> his zeal; with a shout he will raise the battle
> cry and will triumph over his enemies.*
> *— Isaiah 42:13*

> *To say to the captives, "Come out,"
> and to those in darkness, "Be free!"*
> *— Isaiah 49:9*

> *Who can snatch the plunder of war from the
> hands of a warrior? Who can demand that a tyrant
> let his captives go? But the Lord says, "The captives
> of warriors will be released, and the plunder of
> tyrants will be retrieved. For I will fight those
> who fight you, and I will save your children."*
> *— Isaiah 49:24-25 (NLT)*

Jesus is still the Breaker Up today!

- He is still the One who will open up a way and overcome all obstacles
- He is still the One who will lead our prodigals out of prison, darkness, and exile
- He is still the One who will raise the battle cry and triumph over His enemies
- He is still the One who fights for us

Again and again I see how our prodigals parallel the Israelites—how much God loves them and longs for their return. How He sends individuals into their lives to speak His words of truth and love; how He waits patiently, wanting them to repent so He can ultimately restore them.

We don't pray to a weak or unwilling heavenly Father. We pray to a *Breaker Up* God!

Prayer Challenge – Day 24

WE WAIT FOR YOU

But he didn't answer her at all. And his disciples came and urged him, saying, "Send her away, for she keeps shouting after us."
– Matthew 15:23

Is that how you feel sometimes? Lord, I'm asking and asking You to bring my prodigal back to You, yet it seems like You are silent. I see no progress, or I think maybe I see something positive and I give You thanks, but then things become worse again. It's so hard Lord. I know what I am asking for is good and in line with Your heart. I know that You truly love them.

The woman in this story knew what it was like to experience Jesus' silence. It seemed as if she was getting nowhere, but her persistence could not be denied. It all started when she came to Him, pleading in a loud voice, "Lord, Son of David, have mercy on me! My daughter is suffering from demon-possession."

Jesus didn't respond.

She must have said it more than once and we know it was bothering the disciples (sometimes I'm amazed by their lack of compassion) because they urged Jesus to send her away.

Then Jesus spoke, yet His words were not very encouraging: *"I was sent only to the lost sheep of Israel"* (Matthew 15:24)—which is true in the sense that salvation didn't come to the Gentiles until after Jesus returned to heaven.

But the mother wouldn't take "No" for an answer. She knelt before Him saying, "Lord, help me!"

What Jesus said next seems downright hurtful and disrespectful, but it really was in line with the culture. She was not offended when He told her, "It's not right to take the children's bread and toss it to the dogs."

In her response, she didn't miss a heartbeat. The woman actually agreed with what He said, yet it didn't mean He wouldn't help her. She replied, *"Yes it is, Lord...but even the dogs eat the crumbs that fall from their master's table"* (verse 27).

Now this was faith! I wonder if I would have had the courage to persist in what looked like a "No" answer, but really wasn't. We know this because Jesus told her she had great faith and that her request would be granted. Her daughter was healed that very hour.

Apparently her persistence is what Jesus was looking for in this situation. Salvation had not been brought to the Gentiles yet and the reference He made to her being a dog was a term used by Jews to describe the spiritual condition of the Gentiles. It was not offensive, just a fact.

Salvation would soon come to the Gentiles and Scripture records how Jesus loved them and performed many miracles in Gentile regions.

Like this Canaanite woman, we must not be deterred; we must boldly stand and never give up:

- Even when it appears nothing is happening and Jesus is silent
- Even when we're tempted to feel like we are not good enough
- Even when it looks like the answer might be "No!"

Keep asking, keep praying, keep trusting, keep watching, and never ever think God doesn't care. Ask for His grace in the days, months, even years of waiting. Place your hope in the Lord and look to

Scripture for encouragement and God's heart—as found in these verses:

> *Those who know your name will trust in you, for you, Lord, have never forsaken those who seek you.*
> *– Psalm 9:10*

> *And now, O Lord, for what do I wait? My hope is in you.*
> *– Psalm 39:7*

> *Therefore, behold, I will allure her, and bring her into the wilderness, and speak tenderly to her. And there I will give her her vineyards and make the Valley of Achor a door of hope..."*
> *– Hosea 2:14-15*

> *Yet the Lord longs to be gracious to you; therefore he will rise up to show you compassion. For the Lord is a God of justice. Blessed are all who wait for him!*
> *– Isaiah 30:18*

> *I am counting on the Lord; yes, I am counting on him. I have put my hope in his word.*
> *– Psalm 130:5*

Prayer Challenge – Day 25

JESUS IS THE LIGHT

But you are a chosen people, a royal priesthood, a holy nation, a people belonging to God, that you may declare the praises of him who called you out of darkness into his wonderful light.
– 1 Peter 2:9

God, I thank you for bringing us out of the darkness of this world and into Your glorious light. This is what we want for our prodigals too, Lord. We want them to praise You because they too have been called out of the night and into the day. Then they will say...

Do not gloat over me, my enemy! Though I have fallen, I will rise. Though I sit in darkness, the Lord will be my light...He will bring me out into the light; I will see his righteousness.
– Micah 7:8-9

You are my lamp, O Lord; the Lord turns my darkness into light.
– 2 Samuel 22:29

> *The Lord is my light and my*
> *salvation—whom shall I fear?*
> – Psalm 27:1

Dear heavenly Father, we know that even the blackest of circumstances are not dark to You (Psalm 139:12). You are the light, and in You there is no night at all (1 John 1:5).

Lead our prodigals home so they too will know that they are children of the day; and that they no longer belong to the gloom of darkness (1 Thessalonians 5:5). Then they will walk in Your brightness and declare that You have delivered them from death and kept their feet from stumbling (Psalm 56:13).

They will joyfully give thanks to You for rescuing them from the dominion of the the evil one, bringing them into the radiant kingdom of the Son You love (Colossians 1:13)

> *You are resplendent with light, more*
> *majestic than mountains rich with game.*
> – Psalm 76:4

"Lord, You wrap Yourself in light, and darkness tries to hide. It trembles at Your voice" (words from *How*

Great is Our God by Chris Tomlin) because You are the One who makes the darkness flee.

You show up in a thousand different ways. Keep appearing Lord until they see Your radiant presence. Send Your Word to them; it is a lamp to their feet and a light to their path (Psalm 119:105).

The unfolding of Your words gives illumination and understanding to the simple (Psalm 119:130). What Your Word declares will not return to You empty but will accomplish what You desire and achieve the purpose for which it was sent (Isaiah 55:11).

> *Let the light of your face*
> *shine upon us, O Lord.*
> *– Psalm 4:6*

Prayer Challenge – Day 26

TENDERLY

A bruised reed he will not break, and a smoldering wick he will not snuff out...
– Isaiah 42:3

Jesus came to restore that which was broken (Luke 4:18) and to seek and save that which was lost (Luke 19:10).

Have you ever wondered why the Son of God was so harsh with the Pharisees and so tender and compassionate with the "sinners" like Zacchaeus or the woman at the well? He called one group "whitewashed tombs and hypocrites" and "children of the devil," while to others He said, "Neither do I condemn you, go and sin no more" or "I'm coming to your house today."

Jesus asked the Samaritan woman for a drink of water and then engaged her in a conversation about *living* water. To the woman who was caught in the sin of adultery, the Lord was kind and didn't condemn her. They were all sinners, but there was something different about the ones with whom He was gentle.

I think the above passage speaks to why. This was a prophecy about the Messiah. I love what the Pulpit commentary says concerning today's key verse.

> *Egypt was compared to a "bruised reed" by Sennacherib (Isaiah 36:6) as being untrustworthy and destitute of physical strength; but here the image represents the weak and depressed in spirit, the lowly and dejected. Christ would deal tenderly with such, not violently.*
>
> *Smoking flax shall he not quench; rather, the wick which burns dimly he shall not quench. Where the flame of devotion burns at all, however feebly and dimly, Messiah will take care not to quench it. Rather he will tend it, and trim it, and give it fresh oil, and cause it to burn more brightly. He shall bring forth judgment unto truth. But with all this tenderness, this "economy," this allowance for the shortcomings and weaknesses of individuals, he will be uncompromising in his assertion of absolute justice and absolute truth.*
>
> *He will sanction nothing short of the very highest standard of moral purity and excellence.*

(For an instance of the combination of extreme tenderness with unswerving maintenance of an absolute standard, see John 8:8.)

If your prodigal has even the spark of a flame left, Jesus will not extinguish it. He will deal with the smouldering embers tenderly. He will tend to and fan it back into a burning flame. Once more, do not despise small beginnings; trust God to rekindle the fire.

Maybe your prodigal resembles a bruised reed, who lost his faith because of doubts, fear or confusion. He believed the lies of the enemy, but Jesus is dealing gently with him/her. The compassion He feels is real and powerful.

Just as Jesus wept over Jerusalem, He is weeping over those who are "bruised" and those who are too easily swayed by the world because they don't understand or they are lacking in confidence. Trust God to deal lovingly and gently, and not condemn them.

Jesus said to the wind and the storm, "Quiet! Be still!"—and the storm was hushed. Nothing is impossible with God (Luke 1:37).

Lord, today I pray that our prodigals would grasp

how wide, long, high, and deep is Your love for them, a love that surpasses knowledge (Ephesians 3:18) and that Your tender care would fan their smoldering wick back into a flame.

I remember singing this hymn growing up but now it has so much more meaning to me than it did back then. Here is the first verse and the chorus:

> *Softly and tenderly Jesus is calling,*
> *Calling for you and for me;*
> *See, on the portals He's waiting and watching,*
> *Watching for you and for me.*
> *Refrain:*
> *Come home, come home,*
> *You who are weary, come home;*
> *Earnestly, tenderly, Jesus is calling,*
> *Calling, O sinner, come home!*

Prayer Challenge – Day 27

GOD'S ARMOR

Put on the full armor of God so that you can take your stand against the devil's schemes.
– Ephesians 6:11

This verse counsels us to put on the *full* armor of God not just one or two pieces. This armor belongs to the Almighty.

In Day 18 we learned that when the Lord could not find anyone to intercede on the Israelites' behalf (Isaiah 59:17), God put on His own armor and marched into battle Himself—to destroy the enemy, protect His people, and glorify His name.

When it comes to our prodigals, the Lord has found someone to intercede, in fact "many" someones. Looking at the example in Isaiah 59, plus the story of David and Goliath, as well as the instructions given in Ephesians 6:10-18, we learn more about this protective armor.

When young David decided to challenge the giant, King Saul had David put on his personal armor, but the young shepherd didn't like it—too heavy and cumbersome. In this instance David didn't need Saul's helmet, sword, and shield because he was already wearing the armor of God.

> *You come to me with a sword,*
> *a spear and a javelin, but I come to you in*
> *the name of the Lord Almighty, the God of the*
> *armies of Israel, whom you have defied.*
> *– 1 Samuel 17:45*

Can you visualize David with the belt of truth and breastplate of righteousness firmly in place? Possibly the shoes of the gospel of peace because his shoes took him where he needed to be (he was prepared). The end result would be peace for the Israelites and glory to God.

> *This day the Lord will deliver you*
> *into my hand and I will strike you down*
> *and cut off your head. I will give your dead*
> *body to the birds and wild animals and everyone*
> *will know that there is a God in Israel. All those*
> *here will know the Lord rescues his people,*
> *but not with sword and spear. This is the*
> *Lord's battle and he will give it to us.*
> *– 1 Samuel 17:46-47*

That is the shield of faith; his absolute confidence in the ability of the Lord to fight for him. Goliath caused the soldiers of Saul's army to tremble in fear, all but David. His unshakable faith in the Lord fought off any fiery dart the enemy threw his way. Plus, he was wearing the helmet of salvation.

David didn't have a doubt in his mind regarding the outcome, but if he did entertain fear, he certainly did not let that stop him. Just one small slingshot, one small stone, plus incredible faith—and the giant was defeated.

As we intercede for our loved ones, we need to wear God's armor as we pray and believe. Our intercession is opening a way for God to destroy the enemy, protect His prodigals, and bring glory to His name.

It is *"'Not by might nor by power, but by my Spirit,' says the Lord Almighty"* (Zechariah 4:6).

Prayer Challenge – Day 28

GOD IS AND GOD WILL

The Lord your God is with you, he is mighty to save. He will take great delight in you, he will quiet you with his love, he will rejoice over you with singing.
– Zephaniah 3:17

God is speaking through the prophet, Zephaniah, about the Day of the Lord when He will return to judge the earth for their sins, including His people in Judah and Jerusalem. Zephaniah, like the other prophets that God sent, urged the people to repent, to seek the Lord, and to live righteously.

The above verse was part of the prophecy for the future of God's children. The Lord will gather His people and restore them to their land, where they will live in righteousness and safety, and will worship their Creator. This remnant will, in turn, enjoy the outpouring of God's blessings (Zephaniah 3:9-20).

We are also included in this glorious day; we have been grafted in.

This is spoken of in Revelation 19:11-22:5—and what a day that will be!

In his message, "The Lord Will Rejoice Over You" (www.desiringgod.org), author and Bible teacher John Piper focuses on Zephaniah 3:8-20, which describes the wondrous future of the godly. He writes:

> *The first thing to notice here is that even though the amazing promises of this section relate most directly to the converted and restored people of Israel (verse 10), nevertheless it is a necessary implication of the prophecy that the blessings promised flow out beyond the bounds of Israel and include us who through faith in Christ become Abraham's seed and heirs of the promise (Galatians 3:29).*
>
> *Verse 9 shows that God intends to save more than just Jews: "Yea, at that time I will change the speech of the peoples to a pure speech, that all of them may call on the name of the Lord and serve him with one accord."*

How does this apply to our prodigals? John Piper also writes:

> *In Zepheniah 3:2, the problem with the people in Jerusalem is stated most simply: "[Jerusalem] listens to no voice, she accepts no correction. She does not trust in the Lord, she does not draw near to her God."*
>
> *The essence of the sin against which the Lord is coming is self-sufficiency. They won't listen to anybody. They won't accept correction from anybody, not even God. They do not need God. So they don't trust him nor even draw near to him. This may seem like an inconsistency: a self-sufficient rejection of Yahweh on the one hand (3:2), and a dabbling in idolatry on the other hand (1:5). But it's not.*
>
> *There is in every human, I think, a deep longing to worship something great—to have a god or a hero or some beautiful or powerful thing to admire. But there is also in every human the sinful and insatiable longing, too, for self-determination and autonomy—we will do our own thing and get our own glory.*

Therefore, man does not cease to be a worshipping creature when he rejects the true God. Rather he searches out a god in his own image who will give him all the leeway he craves and exert on him no moral constraints of which he does not approve.

Do you see your prodigal in this description? Did you notice that they have a longing to worship, but what or who they have chosen is misguided? But our God is mighty to save.

Cling to the promise of Zepheniah 3:17: God is with you...He is mighty to save, and will rejoice over you!

Jesus declares, *"...there will be more rejoicing in heaven over one sinner who repents than over ninety-nine righteous persons who do not need to repent"* (Luke 15:7).

Now this is worth shouting about!

Prayer Challenge – Day 29

YET I WILL

Though the fig tree does not bud and there are no grapes on the vines, though the olive crop fails and the fields produce no food, though there are no sheep in the pen and no cattle in the stalls, yet I will rejoice in the Lord, I will be joyful in God my Savior.
– Habakkuk 3:17-19

Habakkuk was frustrated. He didn't understand why God seemed indifferent to the evil that was swirling all around him. Why didn't He do something?

How long, O Lord, must I call for help? But you do not listen! "Violence is everywhere!" I cry, but you do not come to save.
– Habakkuk 1:2

The Lord answers Habakkuk, but the response surprises him, and he again questions God:

> *I am raising up the Babylonians,*
> *a cruel and violent people...*
> — Habakkuk 1:6

> *O Lord my God, my Holy One,*
> *you who are eternal—surely you*
> *do not plan to wipe us out?*
> — Habakkuk 1:12

The prophet found it difficult to accept God's answer. Why would He use a "worse" people to punish Judah? How did that fit with His character? He waits for God's answer.

> *I will climb up to my watchtower*
> *and stand at my guardpost. There I will*
> *wait to see what the Lord says and how*
> *he will answer my complaint.*
> — Habakkuk 2:1

Again, God answers Habakkuk. He doesn't explain why He is using the Babylonians, but He does assure him that all violence and injustice will be punished. The Lord tells him to write it down so the message can be seen by others. He talks about a future time when the wicked will be judged and the righteous vindicated.

Habakkuk is humbled when he fully realizes the mighty power of God. He trembles inwardly, his lips quiver with fear, his legs give way beneath him and he shakes with terror (Habakkuk 3:16).

The prophet opts to wait quietly before the Lord and praise Him, even if He never pours out material blessing on His people again—because He is worthy.

That's what it comes down to. God is worthy! Yet He does not condemn our complaints or honest questions. He will hear and answer us if we are waiting and listening. Even when He doesn't directly respond to our requests, He will assure us that He has a plan and to wait patiently because it will happen at just the right time. We know His plans are good (Jeremiah 29:11).

> *If it seems slow in coming, wait patiently, for it will surely take place. It will not be delayed.*
> *– Habakkuk 2:3*

This promise is just as true for us as we wait for God to intervene on behalf of our prodigals as it was for Habakkuk as he waited for God to do the same.

We must never be afraid to be honest with the

Lord, remembering to always come back and praise Him: "Yet I will..." for He is worthy. He may even show up in power that will leave you trembling in awe!

Prayer Challenge – Day 30

OH LORD, HOW LONG?

How long, O Lord, how long?
– Psalm 6:3

There are many reasons we may get to the place where we, in desperation, ask the Lord "How long?" In this Psalm, David asked the Lord how long before he would be restored. He didn't explain what the circumstances were, but we most likely can relate to a time when we too were weary and felt distant from God. We sought restoration.

Another reason we might feel this way is because we pray and pray, yet it seems we see no action on God's part. Our loved one is no closer to God than before. But when there seems to be nothing else, we always have God. He meets us where we are and reminds us:

- His arm is not too short to save (Isaiah 59:1)

- The prayer of a righteous man is powerful and effective (James 5:16)
- His compassions never fail; His mercies are new every morning, great is His faithfulness (Lamentations 3:23)
- He is able to do exceedingly more than we ask or imagine (Ephesians 3:20)
- He will complete the good work that He began (Philippians 1:6)
- He chose us before the foundation of the world (Ephesians 1:4)
- If we are faithless, He remains faithful, for He can't deny who He is (2 Timothy 2:13)

In a recent message, my pastor addressed the issue of why the Lord sometimes gives us more than we can handle:

- It's so we will LOOK UP and depend on His plan
- It's so we will LOOK WITHIN and depend on His presence
- It's so we will LOOK OUT and depend on His power

It is all about our dependence on God. If you read the end of Psalm 6 you will see that, in spite of how weak and depressed David felt, he still trusted Almighty God.

> *The Lord has heard my cry for*
> *mercy; the Lord accepts my prayer.*
> *– Psalm 6:9*

So on days when your faith is low, running on empty, and you struggle to remain faithful, think about the big picture. What do you want for your child? Your loved one?

Do you remember the father in the story of the Lost Son (Luke 15: 11-31) and how he saw his wayward son from a distance? He must have been watching for him every day, unwilling to give up.

God understands when we ask "How long?" and pour out our frustrations and sorrows to Him. It's okay! But His answer is to remind us of His love for us and to turn to Him, to depend on Him, and to find our strength in Him. Because He is faithful; He is love; and He is *for* us.

Father, You love us, You care for those we cherish.

There is nothing that can separate any of us from Your love...not our faithlessness, not our doubts, fears, stubbornness, not even our denial or complacency, and not our ignorance.

You see us in all our righteousness. Your heart is for us, and nothing is too hard for You. We give You praise and honor because You are worthy.

Prayer Challenge – Day 31

IMMEASURABLY MORE

Now to him who is able to do immeasurably more than all we ask or imagine, according to his power that is at work within us, to him be the glory in the church and in Christ Jesus throughout all generations, forever and ever! Amen.
– Ephesians 3:20-21

Sometimes I don't see this verse at work, and at other times I think I do. I open my Bible and read God's promises to me about my son and I can envision him living like that...fully devoted to the Lord. But this verse says that God is able to do even *more* than I imagine; even *more* than I ask.

Think of all the things you are asking God to do— in you personally, and in those who are away from the Lord. Imagine them living the rich, abundant life that Jesus offers.

*The thief comes only to steal and kill
and destroy; I have come that they may
have life, and have it to the full.*
— John 10:10

The NASB version reads: *"I have come that they may have life and have it abundantly."* The original Greek word used in this Scripture is *perissos* which means: exceeding, going beyond; full, abundant, more than. *Perissos* is only used one other time in Scripture and that's in Ephesians 3:20, our key verse for today.

Thank You God that You are a *good* God:
- That we can trust You (Psalm 33:4)
- That You are for us and not against us (Romans 8:31)
- That You are our refuge and strength (Psalm 46:1)
- That there is nothing that will ever separate us or our prodigals from Your love (Romans 8:38)
- That You are able to do immeasurably and exceedingly more than we ask or imagine (Ephesians3:20)
- That You restore what was lost (Joel 2:25)

- That You redeem us from the pit (Psalm 103:4)
- That You came so we could have abundant life (John 10:10)

Our struggle is not against flesh and blood, but against rulers, authorities, and powers of this dark world. We are here to take them back Lord for Your kingdom.

_____ *belongs to You. They have been bought with the blood of Jesus and are clothed in righteousness. They are saints, set apart for You, God; established, anointed, and sealed by You. They have been chosen and appointed by You to bear good fruit. They are ministers of reconciliation and are redeemed and forgiven and complete in Christ.*

We are confident that the good work You have begun in_____ will be completed. We know all things work together for good to those who love You and Lord, we do. Fill _____ with the knowledge of Your will through all spiritual wisdom and understanding so they may know You better.

Let their heart be open so they will know the hope to which You have called them; that they will understand the incredible greatness of Your power for those who believe You, the same mighty power that raised You from the dead. Jesus, You are the true authority over everything. God gave You that authority when You defeated the devil and placed him under Your feet. We have nothing to fear and everything to gain.

Prayer Challenge – Day 32

THE SHEPHERD

If a man has a hundred sheep and one of them gets lost, what will he do? Won't he leave the ninety-nine others in the wilderness and go and search for the one that is lost until he finds it? And when he has found it, he will joyfully carry it home on his shoulders. When he arrives, he will call together his friends and neighbors, saying, "Rejoice with me because I have found my lost sheep." In the same way, there is more joy in heaven over one lost sinner who repents and returns to God than over ninety-nine others who are righteous and haven't strayed away!
– Luke 15:3-7 NLT

Luke 15 includes three parables that are similar, in that they each contain something that was lost, but when it is found, there was great rejoicing.

The first is the story of the Lost Sheep. Jesus was telling these parables to the tax collectors and other notorious sinners, who often came to listen to Him teach. The Pharisees and teachers of religious law were always watching Jesus or trying to trap him. They didn't really care for lost people, only about appearances and keeping track of the sins of others. But Jesus, who is the Good Shepherd, cares very much about the lost, those who are unsaved and those who have strayed, like the one sheep in this parable. Jesus wants *all* to come to repentance.

> *I urge you, first of all, to pray for all people. Ask God to help them; intercede on their behalf, and give thanks for them...This is good and pleases God our Savior, who wants everyone to be saved and understand the truth.*
> – 1 Timothy 2:1,3-4 NLT

> *The Lord isn't really being slow about his promise, as some people think. No, he is being patient for your sake. He does not want anyone to be destroyed, but wants everyone to repent.*
> – 2 Peter 3:9 NLT

God's people are often referred to as sheep (Psalm 23; Isaiah 53:6). John 10:18 says sheep that are not in the fold, Jesus must bring them in. This is referring to future Gentile believers.

Sheep can refer to future believers as well as believers. Sheep can wander away and get lost. This book is focused on those who have wandered away. We are persisting with Jesus since He knows where they are and will go after them until they are back safe in His arms.

We all play a vital role. Our prayers are like roadblocks, slowing the prodigals down, even stopping the enemy in his tracks. Most important, they move the hand of our heavenly Father.

We pray God's Word because:

- It is living and active (Hebrews 4:12)
- It is God-breathed and beneficial for teaching, for rebuking, for correction, and for training in righteousness (2 Timothy 3:16)
- It gives us hope (Romans 15:4)
- It works in believers (1 Thessalonians 2:13)
- It does not return to God empty, but accomplishes what He intends (Isaiah 55:11)

Prayer Challenge – Day 33

YOUR PLAN FOR MY CHILD

And afterward, I will pour out my Spirit on all people. Your sons and daughters will prophesy, your old men will dream dreams, your young men will see visions.
– Joel 2:28

In this verse, Joel is speaking of a future time. We see this fulfilled at Pentecost (Acts 2). In verses 17-21, Peter quotes Joel's prophecy and tells the people they were seeing what was prophesied long ago (verse 16).

I believe all have the ability to prophesy. Many will dream dreams with spiritual significance and some will have visions. God can cause anyone to meet Jesus through a dream or vision just as He did with Saul on the road to Damascus.

When my son was born we gave him the name of a prophet. I wondered if he would move in the prophetic (which at the time I knew almost nothing about). Today, I look at some of the promises God has spoken to my heart and I believe he will be used prophetically and be filled with the Holy Spirit. He will serve the Lord wholeheartedly in the kingdom of God.

Our heavenly Father has a plan for all of our prodigals. Whether you have specific promises or not, you can know His plans are good...to prosper them and give them a hope and a future. You might not be able to see it now, but hold onto the promise! Declare what you know to be true if they are a child of God.

> *"For I know the plans I have for you,"*
> *declares the Lord, "plans to prosper you*
> *and not to harm you, plans to give you a*
> *hope and a future. Then you will call on me*
> *and come and pray to me, and I will listen to*
> *you. You will seek me and find me when you*
> *seek me with all your heart. I will be found*
> *by you," declares the Lord, "and will*
> *bring you back from captivity."*
> – Jeremiah 29:11-14

You may read Scripture that was originally intended for the Israelites, but when the Holy Spirit came, and soon after the Gentiles were grafted in, many promises became relevant for all believers. Since God's Word is living and active, He can quicken it to your heart, and give you the assurance, "This is a promise for you my child" or "This promise is for _____."

God says that when we call out to Him, He will answer and show us great and mighty things we do not know (Jeremiah 33:3). Today, the Lord is saying:

- Taste and see that I am good (Psalm 34:8)
- Find rest in Me alone (Psalm 62:5)
- Run to My name for I am a strong tower (Proverbs 18:10)
- Believe that it is Jesus who will transform your lowly body so that it will be like His glorious body (Philippians 3:21)
- You have been raised with Christ, so set your heart and mind on things above for your real life is hidden with Christ in Me, your God (Colossians 3:1-3)
- Come to Me with freedom and confidence (Ephesians 3:12)
- If I am for you, who can be against you? (Romans 8:31)

For this reason, since the day we heard about you, we have not stopped praying for you and asking God to fill you with the knowledge of His will through all spiritual wisdom and understanding. And we pray this in order that you may live a life worthy of the Lord and may please him in every way: bearing fruit in every good work, growing in the knowledge of God, being strengthened with all power according to his glorious might so that you may have great endurance and patience, and joyfully giving thanks to the Father who has qualified you to share in the inheritance of the saints in the kingdom of light. For he has rescued us from the dominion of darkness and brought us into the kingdom of the Son he loves, in which we have redemption, the forgiveness of sins.
– Colossians 1:9-14

Prayer challenge – Day 34

A STRONG TOWER

The name of the Lord is a strong tower; the righteous run to it and are safe.
– Proverbs 18:10

We are safe when we run to the Lord. He can handle whatever we throw at Him...our fears, our doubts, our complaints, our weariness, our frustration, our sorrow, and the list goes on. The righteous can run to the strong tower whenever they need to feel safe.

My husband makes me feel secure, and I appreciate this about him. But I must admit, there are plenty of things about me he doesn't know how to handle. After all, he is only human. That's why I am so very thankful I have the Lord to run to.

Perhaps you've heard it said, "When you don't know what to do, just say 'Jesus!'" This is true because there is power in His name.

A song recorded by Lincoln Brewster, *There is Power*, captures it all:

*Where two or more are gathered in His
name, He is there
For all who come, who run to Him in faith,
He is there, He is there*

*There is power in the name of Jesus
There is power, power in His name*

*No fear, no lie, can stand against us now,
   He is here
The Word has come to silence every doubt,
   He is here*

*There is power, in the name of Jesus
There is power, power in His name*

*One name, one name can save
One name breaks every chain
One name, always, One name, Jesus
One name, one name remains
One name, we will proclaim
One name, always, One name*

So, we can run to Him with the burdens for our prodigals because we know He is waiting and longing for us to connect with Him. We often wait until something goes wrong to turn to the Lord, but He wants us to move toward Him instinctively, every day for every reason.

We will find more than just safety. We will discover unending love, joy, peace, hope, rest, wisdom, the courage to keep going, and the beauty of His holiness.

If for no other reason, run to Him just to be in His presence. If we only knew the riches He has in store for us, we wouldn't hesitate. All the power we need is found in the Lord, and this is true for our prodigals.

God is waiting to hear us; He wants to know what we are thinking and what we want for our loved ones. Tell Him. He longs to share with us how He feels about them and to comfort us and give us strength. He desires to personally assure us that He is fighting for them—and when He fights, He wins!

Prayer Challenge – Day 35

ALL THINGS ARE POSSIBLE

When the spirit saw Jesus, it immediately threw the boy into a convulsion. He fell to the ground and rolled around, foaming at the mouth. Jesus asked the boy's father, "How long has he been like this?" "From childhood," he answered. "It has often thrown him into fire or water to kill him. But if you can do anything, take pity on us and help us." "If you can?" said Jesus. "Everything is possible for him who believes." Immediately the boy's father exclaimed, "I do believe; help me overcome my unbelief!"
– Mark 9:20-24

Jesus, and three of His disciples, Peter, James, and John, had just come down from the mountain after the transfiguration of Jesus. They returned to find the rest of the disciples surrounded by a huge throng arguing with the religious leaders. When the crowd saw Jesus, they became very excited and ran to greet Him.

Jesus wanted to know what they were arguing

about. The father of the boy who suffered with an evil spirit spoke up and explained that he had brought his son to be healed and the disciples were unable to cast out the demon. Jesus seemingly became impatient with the situation and the lack of faith on the disciples' part, so He called for the boy to be brought to Him.

The father also lacked faith but Jesus responded differently. The dad had enough faith to bring the boy, but not enough to know if Jesus could actually heal him or not. Jesus set him straight, telling him, *"Everything is possible for one who believes"* (Mark 9:23).

Immediately the boy's father exclaimed, *"I do believe; help me overcome my unbelief!"* (verse 24).

Jesus then healed the boy.

Later, when the disciples asked Jesus why they had been unsuccessful, He told them, *"This kind can come out only by prayer"* (verse 29).

Jesus was frustrated with their lack of faith because He had earlier sent them out and given them the power and authority to cast out demons (Luke 9:1), and they had previously been successful (Mark 6:13). But when the father lacked the faith needed, Jesus didn't get frustrated. Instead, He was instructive and the father responded.

Our faith plays an important part in how we approach God in regard to our prodigals. What has He given us authority to do? How should we respond when we don't have enough faith? What do we do when nothing seems to happen?

Faith isn't automatic. It isn't just a word, it is an action—and it increases by spending time in God's presence as well as acting on what He tells us to do. This involves getting to know Him and seeing His power at work both *in* and *through* our life. It's finding out first hand that He will accomplish what He says He will do.

If the Lord calls you to pray, then pray with authority, believing the Word. When you see you are struggling, or have insufficient faith, ask God to help your unbelief (Mark 9:24) and to increase your faith (Luke 17:15) When doubt enters your mind, eliminate it as soon as you are aware. Doubt is from the enemy and we have the authority in Christ to cast it out.

In the name of the Lord, I cut them off.
They surround me on every side but in the name

of the Lord, I cut them off. They surround me like bees, but died off quickly as burning thorns, in the name of the Lord, I cut them off.
– Psalm 118:10-12

In using this verse, name specifically what you want to cut off. God is faithful, and seeing His hand at work will also increase our faith. But we must not become totally dependent on this method; let it be a bonus.

Of course, without faith it is impossible to please God (Hebrews 11:6). It is equally as true that there is no condemnation for those who are in Christ (Romans 8:1). So when you fail, and we all will at some point, DO NOT condemn yourself. Repent and get back on the path of trust and belief.

Everyone has been given a measure of faith (Romans 12:3) What you choose to do with what you have been blessed with will determine whether it grows or shrinks.

If you believe, all things are possible. This is imperative when we go to the Lord on behalf of our prodigals.

Prayer Challenge – Day 36

Two Lions

> *Be self-controlled and alert. Your enemy the devil prowls around like a roaring lion looking for someone to devour.*
> – 1 Peter 5:8

We discussed earlier the importance of being aware of the devil's schemes because he is out to destroy God's family. Actually, he is a roaring lion without any real power except what we give him; He was defeated at the cross.

Our prodigals didn't understand this, and as a result he was able to capture them. Although the evil one is powerless, he is skilled at deceiving and diverting. So we must stay alert.

Today, I was struggling to write this devotional. I was becoming frustrated and my heart wasn't really in the process. Thankfully, I didn't give into this distraction from the enemy for very long. I went to God and cried out to Him. He led me to stop what I was doing and just be thankful. To be honest, it was the last thing I felt like doing. But I did, and amazingly it turned everything around. This reinforced to me that the enemy has no real power.

We have another lion—Jesus. He is the all-powerful Lion of the Tribe of Judah (Revelation 5:5), and the adversary is no match for Him.

When Jesus was sent to earth, He came as the humble servant, as the Lamb that was slain who takes away the sin of the world (John 1:29; Revelation 5:12). He was so close to His Father that He only did what He saw His Father doing (John 5:19). He is the Lion and the Lamb (Revelation 5:5-6) who came from the tribe of Judah and fulfilled the prophecy given in Genesis:

> *Judah, my son, is a young lion that has finished eating its prey. Like a lion he crouches and lies down; like a lioness—who dares to rouse him? The scepter will not depart from Judah, nor the ruler's staff from his descendants, until the coming of the one to whom it belongs, the one whom all nations will honor.*
> *– Genesis 49:9-10*

Because He is the Lamb that was slain to take away the sin of mankind, and because He defeated Satan and death, He now wears the Victor's crown.

Judah's Lion will one day return and rule in the power that is already His. This Lion/Lamb can fight for us and for our prodigals—and we can have absolute confidence that He will win! He will be our help and our defender.

The song, *Victor's Crown* by Darlene Zschech, became a theme for one of our 40-Day Prayer Challenges. You can watch it on YouTube or download it on iTunes. It is powerful and one I still play—and sing along as I intercede for prodigals.

While it is important to be alert to the attacks of the enemy and use our shield of faith to stop the fiery arrows of the devil, it is equally vital to focus on the One who has the real power and is able to do immeasurably more than we can ask or imagine (Ephesians 3:20):

- The One who causes everything to work together for the good of those who love Him (Romans 8:28)

- The One who makes all things new (Revelation 21:5)
- The One who sets us free (Galatians 5:1)
- The One who makes dry bones live again (Ezekiel 37:1-10)
- The One who gives us strength (Isaiah 40:31)
- The One who gives us rest (Matthew 11:28-30)
- The One who teaches us what is best for us and directs us in the way we should go (Isaiah 48:17)
- The One who gives hope and joy and peace (Romans 15:13)
- The One who has overcome (John 16:33)!

Let the evil lion roar, Judah's Lion has already won the victory!

Prayer Challenge – Day 37

Determined By God

*In his heart a man plans his course,
but the Lord determines his steps.*
– Proverbs 16:9

Our prodigals make their plans apart from God; they have free will. But God is sovereign and He determines their steps.

I recently watched a movie about a prodigal son. His father was a preacher, but he left home because he wanted independence, his freedom his way—to make his own plans and choose his own life. Sadly, that life didn't include God.

His parents gave him half of his college fund and told him if he could keep his grades up and make his money last for the first two years, he would receive the remaining funds.

Toward the end of his second year, everything was going great until it all began to unravel. He was kicked out of school and out of his apartment. Plus, he lost his girlfriend and crashed his car.

Life has a way of happening without our permission. But God already knows what will take place, and can use circumstances to turn the situation around.

The son in this movie kept having dreams; he began to realize that his philosophy was all wrong. It became obvious that God orchestrated the things that led up to him getting expelled from school. It was the Lord who gave him dreams and was behind what led to his ex-girlfriend becoming a Christian. By looking at a photo of his family, he thought of them after a very long time.

That's when he decided to return home. Not only that, he turned his life over to God and discovered the freedom he was looking for all along. It was a happy ending, one that mirrored the story of the Prodigal Son as told in Luke 15:11-32.

It may seem like your prodigal is so far away and out of reach, but circumstances can change in an instant. God is orchestrating things right now in our prodigals' lives. I see it happening in my son's life. I am praying that he will turn to God in the face of the difficulties he's encountering, but it is still his choice. I believe the Lord will continue to pursue him because he is a lost sheep, and deeply loved by his heavenly Father. The same is true for each one we are interceding for. We don't know when or how it will happen, but we pray persistently, and trust God to determine their steps!

> *God, we pray that the message of the Lord may spread rapidly and be honored wherever it goes (2 Thessalonians 3:1) and especially in the lives of our prodigals...those who walked away and those who don't know You yet. Bring people into their lives everywhere they go, who are sincere believers and will love them unconditionally.*
>
> *We pray these believers will share Your love and truth with them and what they say will be clear and irresistible and our prodigals will respond to You. Lord, we ask that the sword of the Spirit, which is the Word of God, will be wielded often in the presence of our prodigals and those they associate with to strike their hearts and minds and call them to repentance*

and salvation.

Thank You Jesus for loving them enough to pursue them. Thank You Father that You are the One who determines their steps!

Prayer Challenge – Day 38

BEING SIFTED

> *"Simon, Simon, Satan has asked to sift you as wheat. But I have prayed for you, Simon, that your faith may not fail. And when you have turned back, strengthen your brothers."*
> – Luke 22:31-32

The verse from Day 37 reads: "In his heart a man plans his course, but the Lord determines his steps." That's what was happening here. When Peter said, "I will not deny you"…he was planning his course. But the Lord was determining his steps; it was His will that Peter be sifted by Satan and He knew that meant three denials.

In a sense, Peter didn't choose to deny the Lord, neither was it cowardice; it was predicted. It would appear he had no choice, yet from his standpoint, no one forced him to deny Christ. He just did it. He was shocked by his actions, but didn't seem to realize it until he heard the cock crow and remembered what Jesus had told him just a few hours earlier he would do. Peter went out and wept bitterly.

Most important, we see that Jesus had prayed for Peter, that his faith would not fail. There might have only been a flicker, a "smoldering wick" as Isaiah 42:3 puts it, but it would not be extinguished; God would not "snuff it out"; He would tend to it and make sure he had opportunity to come back. And did he ever!

Peter not only strengthened the other disciples, he became the first post-cross evangelist. God did immeasurably more than Peter could have imagined, turning his failure into something extraordinary.

Our prodigals are being sifted as wheat. The circumstances may look different and there may have been no forewarning of what was coming, but they are being sifted all the same. Satan is out to destroy and confuse them, to deceive them into believing as many lies as he can. Thankfully, our prayers are frustrating the enemy's plans, so we must not give up. We never know when their return might take place, and we don't want to miss such a glorious moment. Of course, we want it to occur sooner rather than later, and our prayers can speed up the process.

Yes, it will happen in God's timing, but our prayers are a part of that timing. And just as Peter's denial was used for God's purposes, so will our prodigals'. They too, will be able to strengthen their brothers in Christ when they return, and so much more.

> *Father, Satan is sifting _____ as wheat. His plans are to kill, steal and destroy ____ ...so that every ounce of his/her faith will fail. But we are praying Lord; do not let ____ 's faith fail. It may only be a smoldering wick, but You, Father, promise not to snuff it out, so that when _____ returns, he/she will be able to strengthen others and be used for Your purposes.*

Prayer Challenge – Day 39

OUR WAR

*At the very moment they began to
sing and give praise, the Lord caused...*
– 2 Chronicles 20:22

The Lord was angry with King Jehoshaphat. He made an alliance with King Ahab by having his son marry King Ahab's daughter. So, when messengers came to tell Jehoshaphat that the armies were approaching and declaring war, Jehoshaphat was afraid. He resolved to go before the Lord and he proclaimed a fast for all of Judah.

I love that he didn't let the fact that he had sinned against the Lord keep him from approaching God in his time of need. He didn't try to hide from the Lord. In his prayer, Jehoshaphat did several things:

- Proclaimed who the Lord was (verse 6)
- Reminded God of what He had done in the past (verses 7-10)

- Admitted his absolute dependence on the Almighty (verse12)

The Spirit of the Lord then came upon Jahaziel, one of the men present, and he said that God would fight for them and they would win! (verses.15-17).

The next morning Jehoshaphat encouraged the people of Judah and appointed singers to walk ahead of the army. At the very moment they began to sing and give praise, the Lord caused the enemy armies to start fighting each other. By the time the army of Judah arrived on the scene, the enemy forces were all dead. Not a single one of them escaped (verses 20-24).

We too are at war—fighting for the lives of our prodigals. I think Jehoshaphat's strategy is a winning one for any battle: through fasting, praying, including others, praise, and thankfulness. His prayer is also an excellent model for us:

> *"O Lord, God of our ancestors, you alone are the God who is in heaven. You are ruler of all the kingdoms of the earth. You are powerful and mighty; no one can stand against you!*
> – 2 Chronicles 20:6 NLT

God is the same yesterday, today and forever. In Jehoshaphat's prayer, nothing he said about who the Lord is has changed.

> *"O our God, did you not drive out those who lived in this land when your people Israel arrived? And did you not give this land forever to the descendants of your friend Abraham? Your people settled here and built this Temple to honor your name. They said, 'Whenever we are faced with any calamity such as war, plague, or famine, we can come to stand in your presence before this Temple where your name is honored. We can cry out to you to save us, and you will hear us and rescue us.'"*
> – 2 Chronicles 20:7-9

Are there things God did in the past for your prodigal? Are there promises He has given you? There are certainly promises and assurances in the Bible that we can claim. And whenever we want, we can go before the throne of grace directly. We can cry out to God to save our loved ones, and He will hear us. He will fight on our behalf. Today, and forever, God is for us!

> *"O God, won't you stop them? We are powerless against this mighty army that is about to attack us. We do not know what to do, but we are looking to you for help."*
> – 2 Chronicles 20:12

Like our biblical forefathers, we can put our total dependence on God to stop the enemy. The Father has given us the authority in Christ, but still the power comes from the Lord.

So often we are paralyzed by fear, not knowing what to do, but help is just a prayer away. We can always ask the Lord to help us. He is ready; He is willing; He is able!

Prayer Challenge – Day 40

REMAINING FAITHFUL

***God will make this happen
for he who calls you is faithful.***
– 1 Thessalonians 5:24 NLT

The reason we refer to our wayward children as prodigals is because they have strayed. But remember ...if they have accepted Jesus as their Savior, they are saints. With that in mind, we can pray that they will know who they are in Christ.

It is good for us to see our prodigals as God sees them. We may also be reminded that these truths are for you and me as well.

*Now may the God of peace make
you holy in every way and may your whole
spirit and soul and body be kept blameless
until our Lord Jesus Christ comes again.*
– 1 Thessalonians 5:23 NLT

This is God's plan for us and for our prodigals. The Lord will make this become reality, for He who has called them (and us) is faithful. With our human vision, they don't look like the saints that they are, but that doesn't make them any less in God's sight. They are misguided, and that's why we are praying. We want to see them living out what God has planned for them.

The Lord will honor our prayers; He is listening and will respond. It delights Him to work on our behalf and He is pleased with our perseverance. Like the persistent widow in Luke 18:1-8, His desire is for us to pray as long as it takes.

God longs to show us things we do not know while we are waiting (Jeremiah 33:3). He wants us to trust Him; His timing is always right.

- The Lord is pleased when we are watching
- The Lord is pleased when we are thankful
- The Lord is pleased when we give Him praise
- The Lord is pleased when we know the Word and speak it back to Him

- The Lord is pleased when we want to know Him intimately, not just for what He can do for us
- The Lord is pleased when we look for His surprises
- The Lord is pleased when we seek Him for understanding

As you wait with faith, hope, and expectation, make sure your priority is God.

> *I want to know Christ and*
> *the power of his resurrection...*
> *– Philippians 3:10*

As Christ followers we live by faith and not by sight (2 Corinthians 5:7).

God, we continue to pray by faith, believing that our prayers are making a difference. We pray earnestly for our prodigals like Epaphras, a servant of Christ, did for the Colossians (Colossians 4:12). *We will not give up hope, for hope does not disappoint* (Romans 5:5).

*May the God of hope fill you with
all peace and joy as you trust in him, so
that you may overflow with hope
by the power of the Holy Spirit.*
– Romans 15:13

A prayer for the unsaved:

*Open their eyes so they may turn from
darkness to light and from the power of Satan
to God. Then they will receive forgiveness for
their sins and be given a place among God's
people, who are set apart by faith in me.*
– Acts 26:18 NLT

Acknowledgments

I am so grateful to God for putting it in my heart to start a group for those who have loved ones far from the Lord. He knows I am not quick to respond, yet His quiet and persistent reminders led to the group I now am privileged to lead and the book you are now reading. I am thankful He is patient with me. His love and faithfulness are my Rock. I am also grateful for those who have stood behind me every step of the way.

I want to acknowledge Susan, Lois, and Cindy who separately came and encouraged me to publish this 40-day devotional.

Thank you to my dear husband, Kevin, who has always supported and loved me.

To Contact the Author
Email: lynn.holzinger@yahoo.com
Website: fathersheartforus.com

www.ingramcontent.com/pod-product-compliance
Lightning Source LLC
Chambersburg PA
CBHW071929290426
44110CB00013B/1541